THE JOY OF Decorating

THE JOY OF Decorating

SOUTHERN STYLE WITH MRS. HOWARD

PHOEBE HOWARD

WITH SUSAN SULLY

STEWART, TABORI & CHANG
NEW YORK

DEDICATION

Without hesitation, I dedicate this book to my husband, Jim Howard. Not only is he a great husband and father, but he is also my business partner. When I look at the pictures in this book, I am constantly reminded of the importance of his contribution to my work.

We have a divide-and-conquer strategy in our stores and in the projects we share. Jim does the space planning and creates the architectural shell, from the stairs and paneling to the windows, moldings, wall finishes, and flooring. Then he turns these incredibly designed spaces over to me. My job is to create the floor plans and select the furnishings, curtains, rugs, and accessories that turn these spaces into inspiring rooms. How could they not look good? It's almost impossible to fail with this kind of backdrop.

Jim's rooms are very much a part of my decorating. We firmly believe that architecture and accessories make or break a space. In terms of importance, furniture and fabrics fall somewhere in between. We trust each other implicitly and respect each other's judgment and ability. He is the reason I can get up every day and do what I do, working with clients while running the stores on a daily basis. He is supportive and encouraging, always trying to get me to take the next step. If he questions me, I usually listen—there is probably something to be learned from it. We have been married for twenty-five years and business partners for sixteen. We are intermingled in a very complicated and satisfying way. I am incredibly lucky—and I realize it every day.

Without Mr. Howard, I would never have been able to become Mrs. Howard.

INTRODUCTION

I am not an interior designer. I did not attend design school and have no formal training. I have never even worked for another designer. When I reflect on how I happened upon this career, I realize that I did not choose it. It chose me.

I was lucky enough to have an incredible mentor in my life—my aunt Myra Thompson from Montgomery, Alabama. Aunt Myra touched many people in her life, and the world is a better place for having her in it. She was poised and ladylike, but also acutely observant and intuitive.

I always loved to listen to stories of Aunt Myra and the house she decorated as a newlywed. The floors were stained a deep shade of ebony and waxed until they gleamed. White cotton-duck slipcovers so tight you could bounce a quarter off them covered all the furniture. Large vases filled with fragrant white lilies from her husband's floral business stood in nearly every room. I was intrigued by this vision of dark floors, white slipcovers, and lilies. It seemed so basic and simple, yet so elegant. I realized that anyone could live surrounded by beautiful style if they chose to do so.

Aunt Myra affected my life more directly when I was the delicate age of thirteen. My parents had divorced, and we'd moved from Florida to Alabama for a year. I was having trouble adjusting to the move and fitting in at my new school. My sweet Alabama relatives could see that I was struggling and did what they do best: They fed me! Chicken and dumplings, fried green tomatoes, ham and gravy, biscuits—the food was incredible, and I consoled myself with it. I also gained thirty pounds almost overnight.

I was struggling and everyone was at a loss about what to do. But not Aunt Myra. She decided to decorate my room. She painted the walls pale blue. She found an iron bed, which she had sandblasted and lacquered white. She made café curtains from floral sheets, scalloping the top hems and hanging them with light-blue grosgrain bows. She cut off the sheets' borders and appliquéd flowers around the edge of an aubergine skirt for the bedside table. She painted an old dresser with an attached mirror in sage-green strié. A white wicker desk appeared. The final touch was a satiny-blue quilted bedspread.

I can still close my eyes and recall every detail of that room. It embraced me and allowed my wounds to heal. When I think back to the impact the room had on me, I realize how powerful our environments can be. They affect us far more profoundly than we realize. In every room I decorate, my goal is to re-create the same sense of inspiration and comfort I felt in that bedroom. I want to make a difference in my clients' lives—to give them what they hope for and dream of in their surroundings.

I did not find my calling until after raising four children with my husband, Jim, a designer with a thriving career in architectural interiors and decorating. Throughout most of our marriage, I stayed at home with the kids, but I always kept an eye on Jim's business, observing from afar. By the time our youngest child started first grade, I was ready to launch a business of my own.

In 1996, Jim and I purchased a condemned building in Jacksonville, Florida, and transformed it into the first Mrs. Howard store. Our idea was to remodel the 1920s grocery story to create a retail space that felt like a grand Southern home with fully furnished room vignettes. The finished store included living rooms, dining rooms, libraries, and bedrooms, each completely decorated, right down to the artwork and accessories.

My goal was not only to sell individual pieces of furniture and accessories, but also to inspire customers in their decorating projects. Some shoppers came in to buy just one or two pieces, others ordered the entire contents of a room, and some just ended up sitting and chatting as though they were at home. I loved it when that happened.

The store was an overnight success, and we realized that we had created something far beyond what we had envisioned. After five years, we decided to open another store called Max and Company, named after my son, that targeted a different customer—younger, more casual—the kids of Mrs. Howard's clientele. They worked so well together that we added another location with side-by-side stores in Jacksonville Beach, and then expanded to Atlanta, and ultimately to Charlotte.

The stores became my training ground—a constantly evolving design laboratory. I arranged the rooms over and over again, creating different scenarios that gave me the opportunity to learn about scale and proportion, color, texture, curtains, upholstery, and accessories. I was able to discern quickly what worked and what didn't by the speed with which something sold. If something sold immediately, I knew I'd done it right.

One day, without giving it much thought, I decided to start decorating. I stood by the front door of our Jacksonville Beach store and said, "I'm going to take the next customer who walks in as my first client." Within five minutes a couple entered, and unbelievably, they became my greatest clients—and friends, as well. Since then, I've decorated eight more projects for them. The first one landed on the cover of *House Beautiful*, where it was featured in a twelve-page spread. That really got my attention. A new chapter of life began, and I've never looked back.

Working in the stores over the years, I've learned a lot about how frustrated and overwhelmed most people feel about decorating their homes or even just shopping for furniture. I've listened to customers' concerns, hearing the same questions again and again. How do I start? How do I know what my style is? What goes with what? Can I use any of my own things? How much will it cost? How long will it take? Is this a good investment? What if I don't like it?

With this book, my aim is to replace this confusion with a confident style that's a reflection of individual personality and lifestyle. I've combined pictures of rooms designed for clients with rooms from the Mrs. Howard stores. Together, they illustrate seven themes: Inviting, Inspiring, Timeless, Graceful, Tranquil, Casual, and Comfortable. All of these words have been used to describe my style of decorating. They also describe the many different ways we want our houses to look and feel.

There is another unspoken theme running through this book—the marriage of beauty and practicality. As a stay-at-home mother for eleven years, I learned that it's not enough for a house to look good—it's got to live well, too. Striving to combine beauty with practicality became my obsession, first as a storeowner and then as a decorator. "Keep it pretty" is my mantra. But I also understand the wear-and-tear a family can inflict on furnishings and I keep that at the forefront of my mind. I want to be sure my choices are suitable to the needs of my clients. Perhaps I am practical to a fault, but this gives my work a natural look of comfort and relaxed elegance devoid of pretension and arrogance.

The pleasure of living in a well-decorated space is undeniable. The places we live in should suit our lifestyles, express our personalities, make us glad to be home, and even happier to spend time there. I believe the process of decorating should be just as pleasurable as the finished product. It should be joyful, fun, and free of fear and trepidation.

For many people, this prospect seems daunting. Get help if you can't do it alone—there's no shame in that. A good decorator will help you find your inspiration and make decisions that will bring it to life. The most important thing is to embrace the joy of decorating. You'll reap the benefits of a pretty home that's inviting, comfortable, and tailor-made to suit your lifestyle for a long time to come.

Inviting

$\mathcal{I}$ have a clear memory of the most inviting space I've ever been in. Jim and I were married on Valentine's Day in 1986, and we honeymooned for two weeks in England. We rented a car and traveled through the countryside, changing hotels every few nights. Halfway through our trip, we went to Bath. Driving through the city at night, we got lost. When we finally arrived at our hotel, cold, tired, and hungry, the friendly staff upgraded us to a suite.

I'll never forget entering that magical space. It was a large room with a comfortable seating area and a canopy bed. There was a fire blazing in the fireplace, dim lights, soft music, a bottle of champagne in a silver ice bucket, and a beautiful flower arrangement. The room took us by the hand and pulled us in—which is exactly what an inviting house should do.

First impressions are essential when it comes to making guests feel at home. That's why front doors and entrance halls are so important—getting the details right sets the tone for the rest of the house. Though it might seem obvious, you'd be surprised by the effect polished door hardware and clean windows (or the lack thereof) will have on how welcome visitors feel.

PASSAGES CAN HAVE A PRESENCE

PREVIOUS PAGE: *This service hall connects the mudroom with the main part of the house, offering a great view of the beautiful staircase just ahead. The vaulted ceiling, tall wainscot paneling, and oversize wall lanterns give the space a lot of personality. Even though you only spend a brief amount of time here, it leaves an impression.*

An inviting house embraces you.

Inside the door, greet guests with a fragrance—fresh flowers or a scented candle—and soft lighting from multiple sources.

In an inviting house, each room should compel you to use it the way it's meant to be used. Libraries should make you want to sit down with the newspaper, curl up with a book, or relax over after-dinner drinks. I prefer them to be intimate, cozy, and a bit dark—perhaps paneled. Living rooms, on the other hand, should be luminous and expansive. While they should never have an off-limits vibe, they're best reserved for civilized gatherings. I like to envision living rooms filled with adults engaged in animated conversation while children peek in through the stair railings.

Ironically, the dining room is often the most uncomfortable space in the house, even though guests should feel like they never want to leave the table. I'm a big fan of fully upholstered dining chairs, pretty chandeliers on dimmers, and plenty of candles. Don't overlook small gestures like putting out a white tablecloth for a daytime meal or using your best china every day. Making routine meals feel more like special occasions ensures that the dining room, which usually takes up valuable real estate in your house, gets regular use.

Because we spend so much time in our bedrooms, they need to be treated with importance. Don't hesitate to embrace your feminine side. Most men, although they won't admit it, like feminine bedrooms in the same way that they like women. I advise clients to make sure that the prettiest part of the bedroom, which is usually the bed, can be seen from the room's door. You'll never question whether a beautiful bed covered with luxurious bedding was worth the extra investment and effort.

When I went back to that hotel suite in Bath ten years after Jim and I were married, I was shocked to discover how ordinary it was. I knew right then that it was the small, special touches—the fragrant flowers, the soft lighting, the crackling fire, and the glowing candles—that made us feel so welcome on our honeymoon. Subtle details like these have a not-so-subtle impact. They're your secret weapons. Use them to their fullest effect.

It's never intimidating or overdramatic

FOYERS AND HALLWAYS
An Irresistible Invitation

*T*he foyer sets the tone for the house, offering the first taste of what lies ahead—that's why front doors and entrance halls are so important. With an expression of hospitality, quickly followed by intrigue, each foyer has a distinct personality of its own, whether a warm welcome or a show-stopping statement. Foyers should be well lit and not too crowded—a table with a lamp, a mirror to check your lipstick, and perhaps a chair or two are all you need.

It is essential to pay close attention to the shapes, flooring, wall finishes, and lighting you select. Circular and octagonal foyers give guests inviting glimpses into several rooms, while straight hallways lead them into the center of the house. Cleverly detailed flooring is one of the best ways to give entrance halls more importance and delineate them from adjoining rooms. When stairs are part of an entrance hall, careful consideration of the banister and railing is of primary importance. A beautiful runner held in place with brass rods or well-chosen artwork hung on the walls invites you to climb the stairs.

Equal attention should be paid to interior hallways, which should never be treated as throwaway spaces. If they have interesting furniture or artwork that invite you to pause as you pass through, halls can be important rooms in themselves. Because you are dealing with only one or two walls, it's not difficult to create striking vignettes.

MAKING AN IMPACT

This staircase in one of our stores in Atlanta is a particular favorite of mine. Jim designed it to look and feel like a stair hall in a grand Southern home. The wonderful detailing of the balusters, the leopard-print runner, the soft gray-blue walls, and black-and-white marble floors combine drama with quiet elegance.

STRONG ARCHITECTURE INVITES YOU

LEFT: *The many interesting architectural details of a staircase in our Atlanta store lure you up to the next level. Designed by Jim, the pierced wood balusters recall staircases in Swiss chalets.*
RIGHT: *For the entrance hall, we chose an octagonal shape that offers views into three different rooms, enticing you to enter them. When I notice customers lingering and enjoying the details before they pass on to the next rooms, I know we've designed a successful foyer.*

Details in foyers whet
your appetite for what lies ahead

ARTISTRY ENLIVENS HALLWAYS

PREVIOUS PAGE (LEFT): *The oval shape of this entrance hall and the wavelike pattern of the marble floor make entering this foyer a unique experience.* PREVIOUS PAGE (RIGHT): *Designed by Jim, this sweeping staircase in one of our stores offers an irresistible invitation to touch the banister.* LEFT: *The decorative painting in this paneled hallway creates a surprisingly versatile setting for both modern and traditional furniture.* RIGHT: *A faux-marble dado surmounted by panels painted with Etruscan-style motifs offers a perfect balance of masculine and feminine.*

A thoughtfully designed hallway stands up to the spaces it connects

PANELED ROOMS
The Warmth of Wood

Every house should have a paneled room. Wood has a warmth that you just can't capture with plain walls or sheetrock. While there is a common misperception that paneled rooms are only for men, I find that they appeal equally to women. People tend to think of all paneling as dark, but some of the most successful rooms Jim and I have designed are made with bleached or lightly painted wood. Paneling can be stained, painted, limed, bleached, glazed, or lacquered—the choices are endless. I once designed a jewel-box bathroom by applying simple moldings then glazing them with multiple shades of paint for a shimmering effect.

The first step in designing a paneled room is to decide whether the room should be heavy or light, bold or receding. This will help you to decide on the style and finish. When I am designing a paneled room, I evaluate the objects that will hang in it first, then work to design an arrangement of panels that will best fit the art and the mirrors. It's important to note that paneling doesn't have to be formal. Tongue-and-groove paneling on walls and ceilings can create a relaxed atmosphere. Horizontally applied shiplap is another popular option. Because there is no chair rail in this application, you are not limited by the rail's height when placing art.

CREATING THE ARCHITECTURAL ENVELOPE

We have paneled rooms in all the stores—it's part of our signature style. Paneled walls are not just for libraries. What about a dining room in dark wood tones that becomes dramatic and elegant at night? Or a cozy bedroom with painted paneling? The possibilities are endless.

CONTRASTING TEXTURE AND TONE

Paneled rooms are wonderful places for entertaining. To create a softer look than floor-to-ceiling mahogany paneling, I combined horsehair-upholstered panels with stained mahogany moldings in this room. Woven seagrass chairs introduce a casual tone and the geometric carpet adds a modern touch. An English dumbwaiter serves as a bar, with shiny bottles, decanters, and glassware all ready for a party.

Paneled rooms are neither masculine nor feminine. They are universally loved by all who inhabit them

WALLPAPER
AS AN OPTION

This room had little architectural distinction, so I used faux-bois wallpaper with a pattern of vertical grain to add a sense of height. This wallpaper is so effective that you actually have to touch it to find out whether or not it's wood, and even then you're not quite sure because it's textured. The grain of the oversize coffee table complements the wallpaper.

THE APPEAL OF LIGHT PANELING

LEFT: *I like to create tabletop arrangements that combine different colors, shapes, and finishes, like this composition of antique boxes and brass weights atop a nineteenth-century English piecrust table.*
RIGHT: *Although the architecture of this room is formidable, the softly washed oak paneling, casual linen upholstery, and faded Oushak rug lighten and brighten the space. Pools of lamplight, a mix of antique and modern furniture, piles of books, soft throws and pillows—all these elements invite you to sit back, relax, and enjoy the room.*

Bleached, limed, or painted paneling can be traditional or modern in style

PANELING
PAINTED WHITE

Simple tongue-and-groove paneling becomes dynamic when combined with the diagonal line of this staircase in our Atlanta store. Old-fashioned black strap-hinges add quirky personality to the cabinet and closet doors. This is an example of how you can use paneling in one part of a space without paneling the entire room.

SEA CAPTAIN'S HOUSE
A Worldly Collection

An oceanfront house has to function like a beach house, but this one is decorated in grand traditional style. While I was working on it, my clients were sailing around the world, gathering treasures along the way and sending them back to me. Part of the fun of this project was incorporating these objects—as varied as a vintage stage light and a faux-malachite Chinese table—into the design. In honor of their ancestry, my clients also wanted me to integrate aspects of English and Charleston, South Carolina, style into the house, a request that resulted in elegant paneled rooms and a blue-and-white palette inspired by water and sky.

Jim designed the house's interior architecture, creating a magnificent shell for me to decorate. Dark mahogany furniture and lighthearted fabrics in Anglo-Indian patterns combine easily with the painted paneling and handsome dentil moldings. In the dining room, paneling was designed to frame custom-painted mural scenes depicting Florida's intercoastal waterways.

This is one of the most inviting houses I have ever worked on, perhaps because it is so layered and intriguing. When guests tour it, they must be prepared to spend several hours stopping to hear the stories each object has to tell. The contents of the house constantly evoke your interest, inviting questions and engaging you in a never-ending dialogue.

GATHERED TREASURES FIND A HOME

The entrance hall is decorated with painted paneling inspired by seventeenth-century houses in Charleston and England. Hinting at the global mix of treasures found throughout the house, the entrance hall contains an Italian daybed, a Dutch mirror, a Venetian chandelier, and a Persian rug.

A SEA OF BLUE AND WHITE EMBRACES YOU

With several patterns in varying shades of blue, the living room is simultaneously calm and engaging. My goal was to complement the breathtaking ocean views outside the windows while preventing them from stealing the room's thunder. The antique dhurrie rug with a wave motif lapping around its border unites the room with its seaside setting in such a fun way. Keyhole Venetian mirrors flanking the entrance to the dining room provide an imaginary peek into the next room.

THE BEAUTY OF BLUE

To soften its grandeur, I had the dining room's paneling painted in robin's-egg blue strié. Mural panels by Bob Christian combine elements of Canton china, which the English brought to Charleston in the seventeenth century, with the Florida landscape. The antique English mantel adds the warmth of wood to the room, while the Venetian chandelier introduces a graceful, lighthearted note. My clients love to burn fires in the fireplace and light candles in the tall Italian sconces.

A blue and white palette is the ultimate decorating diplomat—it can seamlessly unite opposing styles

THE CASUAL ELEGANCE OF OUTDOOR LIVING

RIGHT: *Deep rattan chairs paired with generous ottomans face the ocean, providing the perfect spot to stretch out and relax, day or night. In the middle of the veranda, a large round table surrounded by comfortable cushioned chairs invites you to enjoy a leisurely meal. I find that round tables encourage everyone to join in lively conversations.* NEXT PAGES: *Of course, my sea captain had to have a mosaic compass pointing due east on the veranda. A rectangular table dressed with a quilt and tall hurricane lanterns creates a romantic setting for dining.*

BACKDROP FOR RELAXATION

LEFT: *In the cabana kitchen, mahogany cabinetry, an oval window, and a backsplash of green-and-white Portuguese tiles balance order with energy. Shells my clients had picked up on far-flung beaches fill green jars on the counter.*

RIGHT: *Leather chairs, a campaign game table, and this vintage stage light are all treasures my clients have collected on worldwide sailing trips. The stage light was a challenge, but it ended up working perfectly in this room.*

Unique treasures collected on trips—
World War II binoculars, a French game table,
a stage light—all find a permanent home

LAYERS OF SOFT COLORS

Decorated in the palest shades of aqua, this bedroom combines a soft palette with strong details. A gossamer Venetian chandelier and walls painted in subtle strié contrast with bolder statements, including a starburst mirror and a painting by Caio Fonseca. A mix of painted and stained furniture combines with the eighteenth-century English pine mantel (RIGHT) to add structure and texture.

Really pretty—never twee, but with just the right balance of femininity and restraint

A PLAY OF PRINTS

PREVIOUS PAGES: *Montages of shells called Sailors' Valentines hang over the bed in this guestroom where variations on turquoise are repeated in a variety of patterns and materials. In the adjacent bathroom, a mural of tropical flora and fauna beckons you to enjoy a long, hot soak.*
ABOVE AND RIGHT: *The tongue-and-groove tray ceiling, vaulted tester bed, and unusual planter's chair with book rest suggest a tropical atmosphere. Contrary to expectation, the many red-and-white patterns calm the space.*

Inspiring

A lot goes into decorating a house—making a budget, drawing a floor plan, finding a designer—but perhaps the most important (and often most challenging) thing is identifying your source of inspiration. When I start a project, I often ask clients to show me a physical object they really love—a photograph, a piece of fabric, a swatch of color. Once a client handed me a page from a paint deck with several shades of brown that I ended up using throughout the house. On another occasion, an antique aquamarine ring inspired a beautiful blue bedroom. I've even decorated an entire house around a single antique blue-and-white-striped textile.

I won't deny that travel is my favorite way to find new ideas. Let's face it—looking for inspiration is a great excuse to hop on a plane for an adventure. Jim and I have regular stops we make on our trips to New York, England, and France. Because our stores offer a broad mix of high and low style, we shop everywhere. In London, we go straight from Carlton Hobbs and Guinevere to Church Street or Lily Road. We never miss the Kips Bay Decorator Show House in New York or the Maison&Objet show in Paris. The great houses here and abroad, such as

LISTEN AND LEARN

PREVIOUS PAGE: *Inspired by memories of my daughter's room, this bedroom for a teenage girl has light pink walls, batiste curtains, and a tufted sofa and slipper chairs. This intimate corner is the perfect spot to read, talk on the phone, or visit with friends. The acrylic coffee table provides a place to put things down without overcrowding the space.*

Inspiration surrounds us all day, every day.

Versailles, Blenheim, and Drayton Hall, are other must-see stops. We often visit the same places over and over—and discover something fantastic every time.

But you don't have to leave home to be inspired. I've discovered that nature is a great place to start. Clouds hold a special fascination for me—their shapes, colors, and moods have launched many decorating ideas. Water, with its many shades of blue and green, is another source of constant inspiration. I once worked for clients who took me to the railing of a boat off the coast of Mustique and said, "Look down, look up. This is what we want in our house."

Make sure the starting point you choose really excites you. I usually show clients many images, watching their reactions until I see what really grabs them. With one particular client, I know not to stop until she gets goose bumps. When she has a physical reaction to something, I know I've got a winner.

Inspiration is double-sided—every room begins with it, but truly great rooms inspire others. I hope our stores are a never-ending source of inspiration for everyone who visits them. The carefully curated rooms are meant to encourage our customers to pay closer attention to the elements of design, to rethink how they live at home, and to find their decorating legs.

Keep track of what inspires you. Start a file filled with magazine pages, paint chips and fabric samples, and pictures of furniture and accessories that you like. You can even display things that capture your imagination on an inspiration board. But keep in mind that translating ideas into finished interiors is not always a do-it-yourself project. Decorating is a profession—not everyone is good at it. If you need help, get it. You'll thank yourself later.

Whether decorating on your own or working with a professional, the most important thing about inspiration is to never stop looking for it. Your house should constantly evolve as you find new treasures that reflect your interests and passions. This will keep it vibrant. The real secret to creating and maintaining an engaging home is to keep asking, "What inspires me?"

You just have to learn to see it

SURPRISE INSPIRATION
The Power of Pink

*M*y inspiration for this room came from a very subliminal place. I was creating a bedroom for a young teenage girl—a place to shelter her from the difficulties of being a teenager. I blended soft pink walls with shiny surfaces and crisp white fabrics to make it sweet, but not childish. When I entered the finished room, I immediately became aware of what I had subconsciously done. My daughter Nellie had just turned eighteen and would be leaving for college in the fall. Without being aware of it, I had decorated this room almost exactly the same way as her nursery. Tears streamed down my face as I came to the surprising realization that I was trying to hang on to her. Sometimes inspiration comes from a place you don't recognize until you see the finished product.

USE PINK IN A FRESH AND MODERN WAY

This room is a sophisticated interpretation of my daughter's nursery, which had light-pink walls, a pale-gray ceiling, and white trim. Sheer draperies, an antique Oushak rug, and a metal canopy frame recalled specific details of her room, right down to the wrought-iron crib. Shiny accent pieces like the mirrored bedside table add sparkle and glamour appropriate for an older girl.

PLAYFUL AND PRETTY

The antique miniature loveseat on the étagère inspired the shapes and colors in the room. White furniture with pretty curves, including the padded headboard and the delicately detailed desk chair, were both influenced by it. This is an example of finding a specific object that you are drawn to and using it as the foundation for a room's decoration.

MAKING A STATEMENT
Rooms Saturated with Color

*D*on't be afraid of color. I have learned to love it. It's the easiest way to make a statement in a room. I'm always surprised by the richness of strong colors and how they can completely transform a space. A deep wall color, whether dark or luminous, makes the other elements in the room—antique furniture, a strong modern piece, or a collection of porcelain—really shine. Strong color is like a black dress that comes to life when you accessorize . . . properly.

Rooms painted in saturated colors usually dictate a lighter shade for the trim. In a living room in our Charlotte store, the color choice was led in part by the classical cornice molding that makes a strong architectural statement. The grand moldings, soaring fourteen-foot ceiling, and tall windows led me to choose a rich mocha brown that is simultaneously warm and dark. I wanted the architecture to sing, so I painted the moldings white. To offset the room's formality, I designed window coverings with a whimsical treatment, sewing wooden tassels onto the points of the valances.

In a dark room, you don't want all the upholstery to be the same tone because then there is no contrast. Everything will blend into the shadows. In our store's brown living room, ivory-colored Tibetan rugs and a creamy palette soften the space while dark wood punctuates it. This large room allows for a variety of seating, dining, and lounging areas.

BOLD COLORS STAND UP TO STRONG ARCHITECTURE

In order to give the grand classical architecture of this room a more modern sensibility, I chose a sophisticated shade of brown. Furniture with clean lines and tailored upholstery balances the strength of the traditional cornice moldings. Wooden chandelier tassels are sewn onto the points of valances scaled to the enormous windows.

PUSHING THE ENVELOPE FOR GREAT RESULTS

In this living room corner, I wanted to combine exotic, traditional, and modern elements. A table by Bunny Williams and chairs by Suzanne Kasler—two of my favorite designers—stand below an antique Japanese screen. On top of a faux-marble mantel, Kudu horns flank a contemporary charcoal sketch by Celia Gerard. A modern marble-topped table forms a striking vignette paired with a nineteenth-century English chaise longue and Regency bookcase.

INFLUENCES AND INSPIRATION
ARE ALL AROUND US

Ideas can come from unexpected sources, as in this dining room inspired by Scarlett O'Hara. With walls upholstered in green velvet and matching curtains, you have everything you need to make a dress, should things go bad. The nail-head trim with starburst medallions led to the selection of the star-shaped mirror at right. This rich green velvet provides a sumptuous backdrop for blue-and-white porcelain and mahogany furniture that absolutely glows against it.

BOLD COLORS
FOR A SOFT ROOM

To contrast with the grand scale of this room, I decided to introduce a more youthful, casual element. These turquoise walls create a vibrant atmosphere and are the perfect foil for furniture in various shades of white and ivory. The distressed patina of painted wood furniture introduces texture while respecting the light palette. The seagrass rug and matchstick blinds add variety.

URBAN LIFE IN A HIGH-RISE AERIE

ABOVE: *In a dark room, details like this stitched cowhide rug and black chinoiserie coffee table really stand out.* RIGHT: *I faced many architectural challenges in this room in a high-rise apartment—strange angles, unattractive soffits, and narrow floor-to-ceiling bookcases. My solution was to lacquer the walls and moldings in a matching shade of chocolate brown. Art, ceramics, and books that might have been lost in a lighter room take on a prominent role against this background. Despite the dark color, this room glows by day and night and allows the contents to express their full personality.*

THE BEAUTY OF BERMUDA
Expressing the Vernacular

*W*hen you fly into Bermuda, you can't help but be exhilarated by the incredible scenic beauty of the island. The bright blue sky, the white clouds, and the clear water are breathtaking. Combined with the romantic appearance of the architecture, this scenery provides a multi-layered source of inspiration. As I traveled to these clients' house for the first time, I thought, *Wow, you really can't compete with this setting.* So my goal became to reflect and complement it.

The shimmering colors of the ocean and sky just outside the windows inspired the blue-and-white palette. The texture and color of the white and pastel walls of the island's architecture influenced the wall treatments. And the Anglo-Indian tradition of using simple yet boldly shaped furniture guided my choice of antique and reproduction tables, chairs, and beds. In keeping with vernacular traditions, Jim designed tray ceilings in most of the rooms, but by using a variety of surface treatments, we created modern interpretations that distinguish this house from its neighbors.

Unexpected elements, including the pebble floor of the outdoor shower room, add more individuality. The idea for the stone mosaic floor came from Greece, where my clients live. Another surprising detail is the richly colored African textile I found to hang in the living room; I only later learned that the wife was born in Africa.

FLOORS AND CEILINGS: MAKING AN IMPACT

The pale pink walls of this indoor-outdoor shower room, designed by David Benevides, are pure Bermudan in style, but the pebble mosaic floor was inspired by Greece. The patterned floor and white rafters of the open-air ceiling turn what would otherwise be a utilitarian room into a magical and unexpected space.

ISLAND STYLE ENCOURAGES INNOVATION

The pale walls of Bermuda's architecture were the jumping off point for the walls and ceilings of this room, but I wanted to introduce a variation. Jim suggested washing the limestone walls and tray ceiling in warm shades of gray to distinguish them from the island's typical white and pastel tones. Similarly, the furnishings' blue-and-white palette departs from the reds, greens, and yellows typical of Anglo-colonial style. In the textiles and Chinese garden seats, I introduced Asian and African influences to complement the dark wood furniture typical of the West Indies.

72

A NOD TO YOUR ROOTS

LEFT: *A boldly patterned African textile adds graphic punch to the living room's blue-and-white palette.*
RIGHT: *The decoration of the dining room is a modern interpretation of West Indies style. Caned chairs were a popular choice in tropical outposts, but I painted them white to give them a modern spin. Bob Christian designed a fanciful mural that recalls the exotic motifs found in nineteenth-century English mural wallpapers. The pattern continues up the walls onto the tray ceiling, visually increasing the height of the room.*

Cultural influences guide us and ultimately help define us

BLUE AND WHITE: CLASSIC, FRESH, AND TIMELESS

PREVIOUS PAGES: *A negative-edge pool melts seamlessly into the beautiful island scenery. Deep-blue garden seats and batik pillows take the surrounding colors and crank them up a notch.* RIGHT: *In the kitchen, a backsplash of polished blue macauba marble captures the shimmering variations of the ocean. Dark-stained floors contrasted against crisp white cabinets reminded me of the juxtaposition of mahogany furniture with white walls found in many old houses in Bermuda.*

NATURAL FIBERS WARM A COOL PALETTE

In the master bedroom, I was inspired by the strong, dark lines of a four-poster bed that seemed to demand a quiet blue-and-white color scheme. Hand-blocked cottons and embroidered fabrics reminiscent of India—another English colonial outpost—complement the West Indian design of the bed. I used a seagrass rug and matchstick blinds to introduce a natural element and paintings by Mary Beth Thielhelm to bring the ocean right into the room.

PINK DRAGONFLIES DANCING

LEFT: *Modern headboards and brilliant colors keep this room for two little girls from feeling too babyish. After completing the room, I felt there was something lacking. During the design process, I had asked Bob Christian to help me put my finger on it. This is a perfect example of how inspiration can come from an unexpected place.*
RIGHT: *Raffia wallpaper covers the walls and ceilings of the family room, giving warm, natural texture and making the ceiling seem higher. Slipcovered chairs and a wicker coffee table create a carefree atmosphere.*

Unexpected color and texture combinations
make a space feel fresh and lively

EMBRACE COLOR

ABOVE: *I felt the need to introduce fresh, bright color into this guestroom.
Inspired by the watercolor over the bed, painted by the client's mother,
I chose a fabric with lime green and turquoise stripes for the curtains.*
RIGHT: *In this little boys' bedroom, the nautical atmosphere directed my
furniture choices. The model boat perched above the bed, the tripod
lamps, and the convex mirror all have nautical origins. The bold West
Indian–style bed was reproduced from a nineteenth-century piece.*

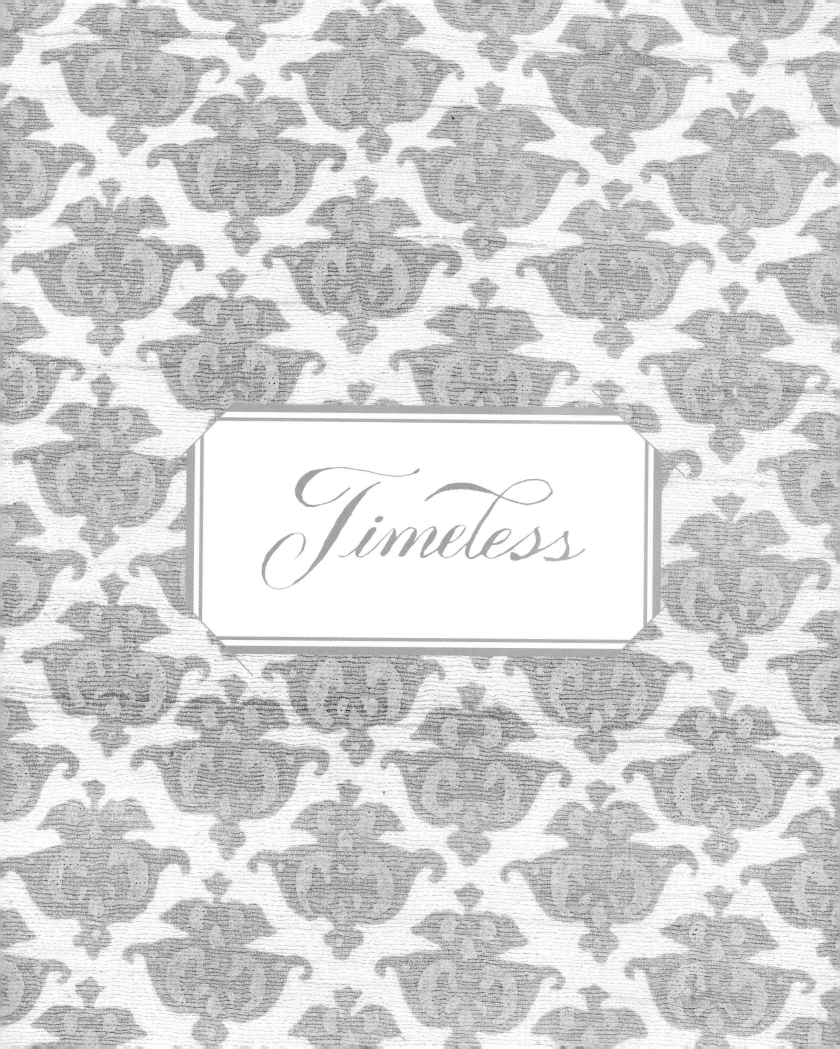

Timeless

*A*n all-time favorite space of mine is the drawing room at Colefax & Fowler's showroom in a nineteenth-century London townhouse. Its classical moldings and plasterwork ceiling are formal and traditional, but chrome-yellow walls and the clever placement of mirrors in the pilasters give the room a fresh, forward-looking style. Lavish curtains of unlined taffeta and beautiful passementerie combined with an ever-changing arrangement of furniture are elegant and casually comfortable at the same time.

When I first saw it twenty-five years ago, this room made an impression that has stuck with me ever since. I've often asked myself, "How has it survived so many shifts in taste and style and still remained so classic?" The answer is that like all great timeless rooms, it's full of history yet entirely current. Unlike a slavishly "modern" room, it will never look dated. It's as relevant today as when it was designed.

PAIRING THE OLD WITH THE NEW

PREVIOUS PAGE: *In the living room of our Atlanta apartment, a thick piece of beveled glass sits on top of an antique architect's desk, giving the nineteenth-century piece a modern look. In another pairing of the antique with the modern, I placed a new brass lamp next to a nineteenth-century barometer, trusting in similarities in shape and patina to create a compatible composition.*

The ability to look at the past with fresh

This is one reason I always recommend being cautious about following trends in a major way. Trendy decorating is like having an affair—it might seem like a good idea at the time, but you almost always regret it. I recently had dinner with a friend who said, "I like trends," to which I replied, "That's why you tear your living room out and redo it every two years." It's okay to embrace fleeting styles in a small way, but not wise to make a major investment in them. Only bring home a few small, easily changeable items, like a pillow, lamp, or other accessories. That way, you can test-drive the current fashions without making a big commitment.

One of the best ways to create a timeless interior is by mixing furniture and accessories from different periods and styles. You never want to let a single one dominate. Antiques prevent modern settings from appearing sterile or one-dimensional. Their handcrafted details add a layer of patina, the romance of the past, and a sense of soul. Substantial, statement-making pieces like a large secretary or a fantastic mirror anchor a room, and smaller pieces, like collections of boxes or pottery, add personality.

It's just as important to incorporate modern pieces into traditional spaces to keep them from feeling frumpy or dated. Two favorite fall-backs are modern coffee tables and artwork. With clean lines and a shiny surface, a mirrored Parsons-style coffee table—or anything made of Lucite, brass, or glass—injects a definitively fresh look without making the room feel cold. Likewise, a contemporary painting livens up a traditional room with color and personality.

Regardless of era, furniture with clean, classic lines is the staple of timeless style. When I'm choosing modern furniture, I look for things with sleek profiles, like mid-century tables or contemporary upholstered pieces, that pair beautifully with the more delicate silhouettes of antiques. For the same reason, I tend to buy antiques with unfussy profiles that fit easily into modern interiors.

Decorating is expensive, so use good judgment when purchasing and buy only what you truly love. Just remember that the key to creating timeless style is keeping two feet in the past and both eyes on the future.

eyes is the secret to timeless style

OUR APARTMENT IN ATLANTA
High Up in the Clouds

*O*ur apartment in Atlanta is a perfect example of how to mix the old with the new to create a space that feels both fresh and traditional. When we purchased it, there was nothing more than a series of plain rooms with unattractive windows and sliding glass doors. The first thing we did was create architectural integrity by adding a foyer, hallways, and deep door openings. Parquet floors and handsome moldings contribute more depth and dimension.

Although the foyer is a small space, I wanted it to make a strong first impression. To make it look larger, I commissioned a paint treatment with barely discernable overlapping squares of blue, green, and beige. Luckily I found a Regency console table only eleven inches deep—perfect for the space and just large enough for a pair of lamps. I added a mirror above the table and Gothic chairs on either side, providing everything a foyer needs without creating clutter.

Our living room has beautiful traditional ivory-painted paneling. A handsome Georgian mirror creates a stately focal point lightened by a modern sofa and Danish coffee table. After I'd selected all the furniture and fabrics, I stumbled upon a checkerboard Oushak rug that was perfect for the space. Its geometric pattern gives a bold, whimsical touch to the room.

NEUTRAL COLORS RELY ON ART AND ARCHITECTURE

It's important for a foyer to have a presence all its own, but also to be a passageway to the next room. In the hallway off our foyer, we painted a pale blue-and-white mural of birds and branches to immediately lead your eye into that space. The mirrored doors of the Regency cabinet add depth to the hall and the vertical hanging of art creates an illusion of greater height.

A POWERFUL STATEMENT IN A PRETTY ROOM

The living room's classical moldings, paneled walls, and gilt-framed Georgian mirror set up the expectation for a room filled with important antiques. This made it all the more fun to choose a mid-century coffee table as the room's second focal point. The simple lines of a Georgian breakfast table and the contemporary track-arm sofa reveal just how compatible different period furniture can be. Despite its modern silhouette, the sleek glass lamp on the table is actually an antique purchased in London.

TRUST YOUR INSTINCTS

In the small dining room, I opted for an untraditional arrangement of furniture, with seating on one side and a buffet on the other. Antiques come to life in this modern arrangement that combines a Regency breakfast table and chairs with a very simple upholstered banquette. This seating arrangement functions well for our life, giving us a place to eat and entertain as well as to spread out and work.

Now is the time for creative, sensible American decorating. Use the tried and the true

REDEFINING A GALLEY KITCHEN

LEFT: *Even small spaces can open up when well designed. In lieu of a breakfast table, I chose a high bar table and stools that are more fun and a better use of space.* RIGHT: *Mahogany cabinets add warmth to an otherwise modern kitchen. Instead of hanging upper cabinets on both sides of the room, we floated stainless-steel open shelving on one side of the kitchen to make the space look larger. To soften all the hard surfaces, I placed an antique Oushak rug on the mosaic marble floor.*

Open up and expand small spaces with
creative design and careful editing

PEACE AND SERENITY

Our master bedroom is a very soft, monochromatic room. Jim and I were on an airplane when we discussed how the room should be decorated. When we passed over a bank of white, fluffy clouds, I told him, "That's how I want our bedroom to look." Pale gray walls reflect light from the large window and create the perfect backdrop for a mix of antique and modern furniture. The scroll arm of the Regency chaise looks like sculpture in this minimalist setting.

OPENING UP SPACE

ABOVE: *In the guest bedroom, soft textures and a pale blue-green palette contrast with wood and metal accents. Sheer wool curtains hang from the four corners of the iron bed I designed for the room. A bedside table and English mahogany dresser add the deep patina of polished wood.*
RIGHT: *An antique French stool seems perfectly at home in this glamorous modern bathroom. Jim designed the vanity and medicine cabinets to open up the space with sleek lines and gleaming materials.*

THE BEAUTY OF RESTRAINT
Careful Editing

Rarely do I find a client with whom I immediately fall into perfect synergy. That was the case with this project in Charlotte, North Carolina, however—and it made for a truly joyful decorating experience. When a client is engaged, but not controlling; trusting, but not unaware; opinionated, but open, it brings out the best in you. I was also fortunate to collaborate with the very talented architect Ken Pursley on this project, who amazed me with his skill and grasp of scale and proportion.

Glorious light floods the house, illuminating the rooms in a subtle way that is never harsh or glaring. A pair of beautifully proportioned curving staircases flanks the entry foyer, creating an impression of stately elegance that is softened by the streaming light. Most of the walls are covered with paneled wood or wainscoting and all are painted a luminous shade of cream. Warm wood, stone, and metal punctuate this palette, bringing it to life and keeping it from falling flat, as neutral interiors easily can.

This house is impressive, but its impact is delivered in measured doses. As it unfolds before you, every room is a discovery. Gentle, quiet, and lovely, it's a perfect expression of the people who live in it.

SOFT BUT POWERFUL

This long foyer hall is anchored on either side by pairs of demilunes and benches and accented by ceiling beams that provide a break from the space's horizontal alignment. An Oushak runner leads your eyes toward a painting by Lois Simon that hangs at the end of the hall.

DIVIDE THE SEATING AREAS

In this large living- and dining-room area, there is room enough for two generous seating spaces. Elegantly appointed with painted paneling and a wood-and-gilt chandelier, the room is also a comfortable place where large groups can gather to watch movies or a football game on a television concealed above the fireplace. It is truly a marriage of beauty and practicality.

PUNCTUATE LIGHT COLORS WITH METAL AND WOOD

ABOVE: *A light-filled recessed seating area is the perfect place to read the paper or enjoy a cup of coffee in the morning.* RIGHT: *The mudroom has a sycamore console with baskets below that hold shoes, boots, and anything you need to stash quickly when you come in through the back door.*

THE HEART OF THE HOUSE IS ALWAYS NEAR THE KITCHEN

RIGHT: *This room, just off the kitchen, is a perfect example of how we really want to live today. It's warm, expansive, light, and above all else, extremely comfortable. Any family would be happy to call this their family room.* NEXT PAGES: *The kitchen is chaste and spare in its design, but it's anything but cold. A banquette illuminated by a linen drum-style pendant light, an oval kitchen table, and upholstered chairs make this edited space feel comfortable and welcoming.*

LAYERS OF FABRIC DRESS A MASTER SUITE

The master bedroom should always receive priority when a house is being decorated, though many couples tend to put it last. Master bedrooms should give you a good feeling the moment you open your eyes in the morning and before you close them at night. In contrast to the white vestibules that surround it, this bedroom has walls and curtains covered in matching beige and ivory cotton crewel fabric. The ivory silk carpet and upholstered chairs add soft layers of texture.

A SHIMMERING SEA OF THE SOFTEST BLUES

This bathroom has beautifully cut blue Celeste marble on the walls and an ivory mosaic marble floor. It shimmers and dances in the sunlight, creating a visual symphony of reflections. Reeded vanities painted in high-gloss blue complement the marble walls and a double layer of sheer curtains allows for different levels of light and privacy.

Graceful

*I*t can be difficult to pin down just what makes a house graceful. You have to strike the right balance between refined elegance and relaxed comfort. Simple design juxtapositions—soft and sculptural, straight and curved, patterned and plain—create an intangible sense of beauty and interest. But beauty in decorating is not just about the individual components—it's about the sum of the parts, the whole composition.

The fundamental ingredient of a graceful home is a harmonious arrangement of its elements, from the furnishings to the textiles to the accessories. While harmony requires consistency and order, a nuanced play of light, color, and texture is just as important. It's not the style of the room that matters—whether pretty or handsome, dressy or casual—but the way in which all its parts are combined.

Creating a graceful room starts with the proper placement of furniture. That's why I always begin projects with a floor plan. Ask yourself how you want to live in a room and how you want to move through it, then arrange the furniture accordingly. But even the smartest floor plan won't produce a

EMBRACE YOUR FEMININE SIDE

PREVIOUS PAGE: *With a shirred silk ceiling, this bed is even more beautiful on the inside than it is on the outside. I love using monogrammed pillows on beds—I'm a Southerner and I'll monogram anything. The handsome engraving of Charles Drouet by James McNeill Whistler invites the man of the house into this feminine sanctum.*

A graceful room is characterized by the

graceful room unless the pieces you choose are in proper proportion—which is sometimes difficult to grasp. The art of balancing the scale, shape, and style of furnishings takes years of trial-and-error to master, but there are a few fundamentals everyone can learn.

Start by considering the scale of your room. One of the most common mistakes is placing too much big, tall furniture in large houses. In grand rooms with very high ceilings, you don't want to base the furniture on the height of the ceiling. You actually need to do the opposite in order to bring the scale down to human size. That's not to say that all the furniture should be diminutive—it just needs to be approachable. Usually, large rooms should be broken into multiple seating areas that create natural places for conversation. At parties, men and women typically split into two groups, as they have throughout the ages. It's nice when both groups have a place to gather and converse. That way, grand can still be intimate.

Symmetry is another important consideration. There's nothing more pleasing than architectural balance, but a room arranged in perfect symmetry is rigid and boring. I'll admit that I love pairs—chairs, mirrors, stools, lamps—but I'm not a slave to them. My rule is to keep the mix interesting and lively by not placing more than four pairs in a single room.

Including personal collections is another way to add vitality, but careful editing is essential. All of your art, antiques, or decorative objects should not be displayed at once or in one room. Beauty alone is not reason enough for each piece to make the cut. Be selective and arrange things in a neat and balanced manner. Order is conducive to a harmonious interior—clutter is not.

Regardless of whether you want your home to be elegant or relaxed, always let comfort be your guide. Choose lighting, furniture, and upholstery that encourage lingering. Nothing is less graceful than a beautiful but unused space. You know you're in a graceful home when you hear yourself saying, "I love being here"—even if you can't exactly place your finger on why you feel that way.

harmonious composition of all its elements

A VANILLA CONFECTION
Soft, Pretty, and Refined

Layers of ivory and cream make this bedroom the dreamiest of retreats. Unabashedly feminine, the bed epitomizes what I think a bed should be—lovely, inviting, and luxuriously comfortable. No bedroom can be truly beautiful without lavish attention to the details of the bedding. This bed has beautifully embroidered sheets and duvet cover, a quilted cotton sateen coverlet and shams, and, of course, monogrammed pillows. I usually add decorative pillows that do not match the rest of the bedding to keep it more interesting.

The bed serves as a touchstone for the decoration of this entire room. The gracefully scalloped lines of the canopy, repeated on the headboard, coverlet, and dust ruffle, introduce a subtle rhythm picked up by the curvaceous French armchair and English stool. And the bed's tone-on-tone palette, ranging from white linen to champagne-colored embroidery, inspired the room's pale color scheme. Faux-shagreen wallpaper, a painted French armchair, and pale-beige upholstery create a seamless unity.

For balance, I chose more masculine furniture that contrasts with the ethereal bed in weight, shape, and material. A gleaming mahogany table stands next to the bed's soft hangings and a modern onyx dressing table with a Chinese bamboo stool serves as a vanity. Framed prints hung in orderly grids give structure to the walls, and brass tabletop objects and a brass fretwork étagère add golden highlights.

MULTIPLE SHADES OF IVORY REFLECT LIGHT

The graceful silhouette, abundant hangings, and soft shirring of the bed's canopy create a stunning effect. I used embroidered linen for the outer bed curtains, and for the inner curtains, sheer silk with a tiny scalloped trim that reminds me of crochet tatting.

STRAIGHT LINES AND CURVES

LEFT: *The curved lines of this French chair paired with an angular onyx dressing table offer a modern perspective. Layered mirrors catch and reflect the light in many directions.*
RIGHT: *Gilt-framed prints hanging above an antique English writing desk combine varied forms and finishes. I love the graceful S-curves of this nineteenth-century English mahogany stool.*

A person with wit and grace is like a breath of fresh air. Think of these qualities when decorating

THE CHARLOTTE WOMAN'S CLUB
Elegance Revitalized

hen we were shopping for a building for our Charlotte store, we discovered a stately 1924 historic landmark. Home to the Charlotte Woman's Club until 2008, it was the site of many weddings, debutante parties, piano recitals, teas, and just about every other social event in the city. We instantly became interested in the building, but learned that another buyer had right of first refusal—and that he planned to tear it down and build a parking garage.

We couldn't bear the thought of such a landmark being demolished and were delighted when we succeeded in buying it. Then we were in, hook, line, and sinker, for a grueling renovation and expansion—just in time for the recession. Somehow we managed to squeeze through the eye of the needle and get the job done. When opening day finally came, the ladies from the Charlotte Woman's Club came out to celebrate with us. One by one, they thanked us with tears in their eyes for saving their building. Charlotte has turned out to be a wonderful, welcoming town, and we are thrilled to be there.

This is now my favorite store. I love the high ceilings, polished oak floors, and tall arched windows of the original clubrooms. Jim's graceful architecture—from the octagonal foyer to the paneled rooms—adds a stately atmosphere of Southern heritage. Glorious natural sunlight floods all the spaces. It is a magical place.

A BEAUTIFULLY SET TABLE IS A SOUTHERN TRADITION

The dining room table is set in fresh but traditional style. Antique plates, a mix of etched and colored crystal, and modern beaded placemats complement one another nicely. Oversize hurricane lanterns and crystal decanters add sparkling highlights against the mellow glow of polished wood.

REPEAT A COLOR IN DIFFERENT TONES

Lacquered pistachio-green walls layered with many other shades of green—none exactly matching— create a harmonious color scheme in the dining room. The blue-greens of the carpet and sage trim on the upholstered chairs play off the lighter, brighter tones of the walls and patterned linen curtains. When I place a range of colors in front of clients and they say, "None of this matches," I tell them that it doesn't matter—just trust me. It will all come together.

126

A GRACEFUL, TRADITIONAL ROOM

The first thing you notice in the living room is the playful shape of the wool-covered cornice boards, which add a witty note to this room. By using muted florals in combination with pastels and creamy solids, deep upholstery, and plenty of pillows, I shifted the feeling of the space over to the softer side. Touches of the unexpected—Chinese garden seats used as side tables and an oversize quartz-crystal table lamp—loosen things up a bit to create an updated traditional room.

129

FLOAT THE BED
IN THE MIDDLE
OF THE ROOM

The bedroom's amethyst and ivory palette blends softly reflective surfaces—a Venetian mirror, mercury glass lamps, a mirrored vanity—to create a fantasy bedroom. French furniture with a mix of straight and curved silhouettes marries well with the contemporary bedside table and miniature daybed. But the real story is the bed, draped with gauzy, unlined curtains, that floats in the center of the room. I decided to position it there at the last minute, and now this has become something I like to consider when designing clients' bedrooms.

IN THE HEART OF EAST HAMPTON
A Family Retreat

*T*his is the house my husband Jim and I created for ourselves in East Hampton. Even though it had the limitations of low ceilings, small rooms, and a funky floor plan, the early twentieth-century Colonial revival house had a quirkiness that is nearly impossible to capture in new construction. So we kept the original house, remodeling and redecorating it to fulfill our vision of graceful yet relaxed American style.

This house is all about architecture—the flow of one room into the next, the proportions of the rooms, the handsome moldings. While some of the rooms are small, the soft light streaming into them from many directions keeps them from feeling overly so. A variety of wall and ceiling treatments play with the light, reflecting or absorbing it to create subtle effects. In the living room, the matte walls are washed with several shades of cream while the ceiling is painted with shimmering high-gloss paint. Although you may not notice it at first, the combined effect creates beautiful visual harmony.

We used many simple, primitive shapes and humble treasures throughout the house to contrast with the more classical architectural setting. In the foyer, for example, I placed a rustic table made from a tree root next to

TEXTURES: ROUGH AND SMOOTH

Graceful interiors provide visual interest by combining order with the unexpected. My husband designed this stair rail, which is a modern reinterpretation of a Chippendale design. A table made from a single tree in the foyer provides an unexpected element right at the front door and brings the outdoors inside.

the Chippendale-inspired staircase my husband designed. I love the juxtaposition of that very rugged table with the refined geometry of the stair rail and the dentil molding above the door.

In the living room, I combined a mix of English antiques with a seagrass rug and ticking-stripe curtains and slipcovers. To balance weightier pieces of furniture, including a marble-topped end table and a George III walnut chest, I placed a Danish mid-century coffee table in the middle of the room and put quirky Windsor chairs in the adjoining hall. These provide delicate, sculptural elements that lighten the look and mood. This room flows into the hall beyond, borrowing the soft glow of its light and framing views of its furniture and artwork.

My favorite room in the house is the dining room, which combines color, texture, and shape in quiet harmony. Placing the sconces symmetrically on either end of the sideboard and centering them in the paisley medallions established a sense of order. Even though the pattern of the linen wall upholstery is bold, the neutral palette keeps the room visually quiet.

A graceful house is a gracious house, so it's important to use every resource to create an inviting and interesting environment. I decided to use hooked rugs because they have such a relaxed, American folk art look. For the same reason, I picked an antique hand-stitched quilt to cover the headboard and pillows in one of the guestrooms. In other bedrooms, checked upholstery and matelassé curtains contribute to a low-key, comfortable atmosphere for guests.

People often hear about Southern hospitality, but they don't know quite what it is or how to practice it. I believe that gracefulness lies at the heart of Southern hospitality. Because care and consideration went into the selection and placement of every object, this house, created by two Southerners, extends a warm welcome to everyone who enters. Elegant, understated, unpretentious, and sophisticated all at the same time, it expresses what I think is the best of American style.

ARRANGE THE ROOM FOR CONVERSATION

*Most of the furniture in the living room is slipcovered in
a brown ticking stripe that immediately strips away pretense.
Contrasting welt adds a crisp note and a touch of tailoring.
A brass lamp and several gilt frames bring polish to the room.*

COMBINE THE RUSTIC
WITH THE REFINED

In the living room, handsome dentil moldings and the natural texture of an abaca rug are the antithesis of one another. The organic shape and texture of the three-legged horn table contrast with the room's shiny brass lamps and bull's-eye mirror. Because this doorway frames a view into the hall, I thought it was important to place interesting objects there, including a tall, slender Windsor chair and pressed botanicals by Lauren LaChance.

ALL IN THE DETAILS

LEFT: *China, crystal, matelassé placemats, and jute-wrapped tumblers arranged on a faux-bois table make a quiet but significant statement.*
RIGHT: *The sepia tones of the dining room's upholstered walls subdue the pattern, creating a strong yet quiet statement. These Regency chairs take on a modern appearance when paired with a contemporary table. The symmetrical placement of the furniture, chandelier, and sconces unites the room's disparate elements in graceful harmony.*

A graceful table setting can combine the simple and ordinary with the lovely and fine

FAMILIES NEED TO GATHER AND BOND

This paneled room has the most wonderful light. It's a joy to sit here in the morning sunlight, whether with family or alone. In the evening, the mellow glow of the pine paneling makes it equally inviting. Faded florals always bring a feeling of familiarity conducive to relaxation and comfort. The patterned linen on the armchairs is reminiscent of chintz, but in a subtle, updated way.

141

THE KITCHEN SHOULD BE THE HEART OF THE HOME

This will always be my favorite kitchen. In addition to having plenty of workspace, there are many places to sit and gather—several stools at the counter, the French farmhouse table, and an oversize banquette just off the kitchen. This has become a popular gathering spot for drinking morning coffee, enjoying a glass of wine, and hosting small dinner parties. It's a perfect example of how to integrate a comfortable seating area into what would otherwise be considered a utilitarian room. Most people are afraid to use good upholstery in a space like this, but we love it and it works.

REINTERPRETING THE PAST

When I found a beautiful antique quilt, I was delighted to discover that it was exactly eighty inches in width—perfect for covering a king-size headboard with enough left over for two pillows. I have always been a collector of quilts and love the interesting stories they tell. I also found a nice home in this guest bedroom for a hand-sewn forty-four star flag. The wedgwood-blue star-print linen used for the curtains contributes to the homespun atmosphere in an updated way.

A STUDY IN CONTRAST

LEFT: *The master bedroom's soaring ceilings dictated the design of this custom four-poster mahogany bed. Pale-blue walls, embroidered linen curtains, and quilted white bedding temper the strong statement made by the tall, tapered posts.* RIGHT: *In the master bathroom, the mahogany vanity, bathtub surround, and bull's-eye mirror make the same kind of powerful statement when surrounded by the light-colored walls and ivory marble floor. This is the yin and yang of handsome and pretty, strong and soft, feminine and masculine that is great for a master suite.*

Bedrooms and bathrooms should be all that
we want and everything we need

BRING LIGHT INTO PLAY

Curtains in a tiny check pattern and a painted spool bed create an old-fashioned look in this guest bedroom. An English side table with delicate legs contrasts with the chunky bed, adding refinement and preventing the room from becoming too "country" in style. Floral upholstery, walls covered with embroidered grass cloth, and a plaid cotton rug introduce pattern and texture in a subtle way. Tones of ivory and soft green repeat throughout the space, reflecting the light that fills this corner bedroom.

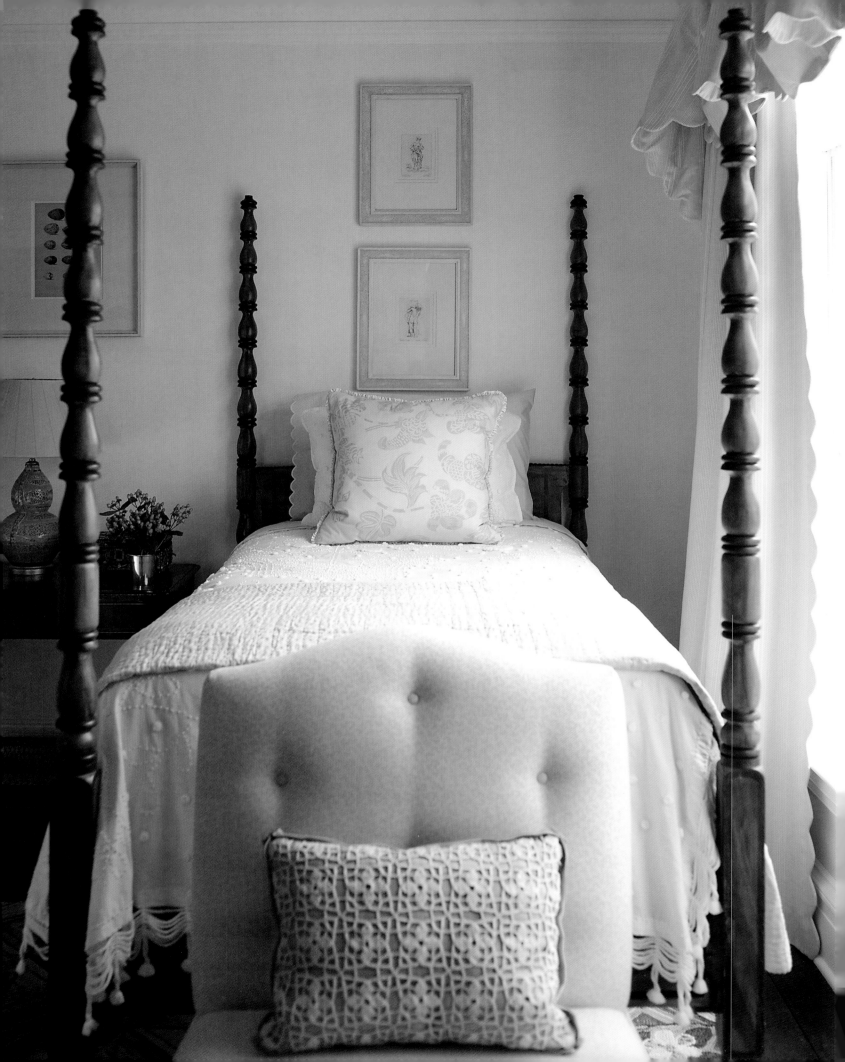

STEP BACK IN TIME

This bedroom reminds me of the summers I spent as a child on my grandparents' farm in Alabama. I selected the four-poster twin beds, rustic chest of drawers, pink curtains, and hook rug from a subliminal, happy place in my memory. Crocheted pillows, chenille bedspreads, and quilts all recall a rural way of life. I scalloped the edges of the curtains and valances to add a simple dressmaker detail. Slipper chairs at the foot of both beds double as luggage racks and a place to sit and tie your shoes.

The most natural decorating recalls fond childhood memories

Tranquil

I crave peace and quiet. I don't watch much television, I rarely listen to music when I'm alone, and I'm comfortable with silence—so it's no surprise that I gravitate toward a serene atmosphere. On the other end of the scale, I have friends and clients who like being surrounded by noise and chaos all day. You might assume that they'd prefer a busy decorating style, but these are often the people who most crave a calm environment. While there are many different ways to find tranquility, I believe the best place to slow down and refuel is at home.

Choosing a soothing color scheme is one of the simplest ways to create a tranquil environment. Rooms with neutral palettes are innately calming. Devoid of competing color and filled instead with a range of subtle shades, these restful spaces are quite literally easy on the eye. I've always loved neutrals, but I've discovered over the years that brighter colors can be just as serene, as long as they are used in a monochromatic scheme. Now I love to take a single color and run with it, repeating it in different tones throughout a room or even an entire house.

SIMPLICITY IS THE ESSENCE OF TRANQUILITY

PREVIOUS PAGE: *The palette of our living room in Jacksonville, combining oatmeal tones with accents of brown-black and gray-blue, is both restful and dramatic. Balancing comfort with elegance, it's a room we visit often, and it serves our needs well. It's like the perfect day-to-evening outfit: Just slip on the right earrings—or flowers, in this case—and you're ready for a cocktail party.*

The best gift you can give yourself is a

Tranquility has less to do with what colors you choose and more with how you combine patterns and shapes. Solids are essential for giving the eye a rest, but a measured dose of pattern can be peaceful, as long as it's limited to one large statement, like upholstered walls or curtains made from a single fabric. Texture is a more subtle but equally important element to consider. What we touch influences how we feel. Tranquil spaces require a perfect balance between the raw and the refined, the sumptuous and the simple. When choosing textiles, study the luster and finish of each, being mindful of how it will be used and what it will sit next to.

Window treatments are essential, for pretty *and* practical reasons. That's why I show so many different examples in our stores. Not only do they frame a view, add polish, and make a room look finished, they also buffer noise, filter light, and provide privacy. Who feels tranquil when they're exposed? Curtains solve so many decorating problems, like disguising bad architecture or making a low ceiling seem higher. It's nearly impossible to imagine a tranquil space without them. I tell my clients, "People who don't like curtains shouldn't build houses with windows."

To create a calming, less complicated space, it's usually best to choose fewer, larger pieces of furniture—even in a small room. The key is to keep the contrast down by selecting lines and proportions that play well together. Above all, creating tranquil spaces is about careful editing. Just remember that liking something doesn't mean it has to be in the room. What you take out is just as important as what you put in. When clients ask for more tranquility at home, I'll often advise them to remove everything from a room and only bring back what really needs to be there.

A truly tranquil room looks effortlessly composed, despite all the deliberation that goes into its design. It's ironic that producing a calm, serene space requires hard work and difficult decisions. But don't let that deter you. The payoff for creating an environment where you can rest and rejuvenate far outweighs the amount of consideration you'll have to put in. Everyone needs a daily dose of calm.

pocket of tranquility in your busy life

OUR HOUSE IN JACKSONVILLE
Water and Light

The minute I walk through the front door of our house in Jacksonville, I feel at ease. It always greets me with a smile, and I'm glad to be home. A moderately sized, two-story Shingle Style house built in 1920, it's situated on the beautiful St. Johns River and is incredibly peaceful and comfortable. All the back windows frame sweeping views, so the minute you enter, your eyes go through the house to the water. The calming effect of gazing at water is undeniable. No matter how hard my day has been, after a few moments of sitting on the porch and enjoying the breeze my stress drains away.

Subdued combinations of colors, textures, and shapes make the interior as calming as the surroundings. We upholstered the living room walls in hand-painted cotton with a pattern that is quieted by soft, neutral tones. Ivory linen accented with touches of blue and brown covers most of the chairs and sofas. This light palette contrasts with the dark-painted pieces and polished wood furniture. We love our art and antiques, and this uncomplicated setting enhances their beauty.

Most of my clients want to line up furniture to face their views, but I don't feel there's any need for that. I experience the view every time I walk through this room and don't think anything is sacrificed by placing

THE FRONT DOOR SHOULD NOT BE FOR GUESTS ONLY

So many people enter their houses through garages or side entrances. I think it's important to enter through the front door of your house and capture the feeling that you've come home. Our foyer has a wonderful curving staircase with a simple banister. The oversize English console table is a perfect example of how you can play with scale in a small space.

Arrange furniture to frame the view by day and be the view at night

furniture in front of the windows. It's important that rooms function the way they are meant to, which is why we put a small sofa facing into the room inside the bay window. When night falls and the view disappears, it provides the perfect second seating area for parties and family gatherings.

There are several rooms in the house that we use in different ways. We enjoy long, leisurely meals in the dining room, which overlooks the river by day and becomes a self-contained, elegant room at night. We prefer to watch movies and read by the fire in the library. Its warm, dusky colors create an introverted space perfect for solitude or shared times with one or two people. The kitchen, on the other hand, is a bright, casual place where everybody ends up at some point or another. Even though there are only two barstools, we're always pulling in more and often end up with six or seven people huddled around the tiny island. Perhaps this is because the kitchen houses the liquor.

Jim and I have always surrounded ourselves with treasures that we gather in our travels—but we've treated them as an evolving collection. For years, we had English transferware hanging on the kitchen walls until I decided that I'd have enough of it and took it all down. I've still got it stored in a cabinet in case I want to come back to it some day. But all in all, we've changed very little over the years, generally only replacing something after it is worn out and not before. That is the definition of successful decorating—being so sure of your choices that you continue to love them year after year. Of course, the fact that we're both decorators helps.

A DAILY DOSE OF CALM

A small curved sofa works well in this bay window. Even though the sofa has its back to the window, the pale-blue shade of velvet unifies it with the water and sky behind. Using the same fabric for the walls and curtains seems to expand the space horizontally, making the room feel larger.

PAY ATTENTION
TO THE CEILING

Jim suggested using high-gloss lacquer on the living room ceiling. By capturing and reflecting the natural light, it seems to lift the eight-foot ceiling high above the room. It's fun, pretty, unexpected, and adds a sense of glamour to the space. The stone fireplace was original to the house. We renovated the house extensively and it was one of the only things we kept. We loved the color of the stone and the intricate carving. Just the right scale, the mantel also makes a high-impact statement in an otherwise quiet room.

160

MAKE MEMORIES

LEFT: *A George III library table is perfect for serving desserts or coffee in the dining room. The Directoire stool looks so modern beneath it and fills the space so gracefully.* RIGHT: *It's well worth the time and effort it takes to set a beautiful table. My daughters have grown to appreciate this ritual over the years. This simple repetition of family traditions is a great source of pleasure and pride. White Wedgwood plates, matelassé placements, waffle napkins, and generously proportioned glasses are among my favorites for setting a table. I never tire of them.*

I try to imagine dining rooms in full swing: candles burning, music playing, glasses tinkling, people laughing and enjoying time together

MAXIMIZE SOURCES OF LIGHT IN A DINING ROOM

Lighting is especially important in a dining room—the more sources, the better. In my dining room, I have table lamps and a chandelier—all on dimmers, of course. I always light candles in the hurricane lanterns, candlesticks, and mirrored sconces. Their flicker and glow bring everything in the room to life, especially the landscape mural. Even though the double-pedestal table seems like a predictable choice, I love the flexibility of seating it offers. During the holidays and parties, we can seat fourteen people around this table for elbow-to-elbow dining that somehow never feels crowded.

164

WRAPPED IN WARMTH

LEFT: *A hallway painted to resemble pecky cypress leads to a family room where we enjoy a fire in the winter.*
RIGHT: *Even though we live in Florida, we always have firewood ready and light a fire as soon as the temperature drops. Jim selected this antique carved pine mantel because its delicate proportions complement the room's cozy scale. Raffia wall coverings and linen curtains and upholstery create a warm, casual setting for relaxing.*

If I had to pick one thing in my house that I couldn't live without, it would definitely be a woodburning fireplace

SYMMETRY AND REPETITION ARE TRANQUIL

ABOVE: *Our kitchen is simple and straightforward—a real working kitchen where many fantastic meals have been prepared. It's usually packed full of people while we're cooking.* RIGHT: *This simple pine table is the first piece of furniture my husband and I bought together after we married. I just can't seem to let go of it. The walls above the breakfast table are hung with postcards written by two sisters on a Grand Tour in 1890. I find this simple grid of repetitive shapes very calming.*

A CREAMY OASIS
OF CALM

When I converted my daughter's bedroom into a guestroom, I chose a palette of creamy neutrals to create a soothing retreat. With minimal contrast in tone and pattern, the surroundings are elegant without being overdecorated. I placed one of my favorite antiques in the room—a nineteenth-century English chair with a scalloped apron and cutout back. Because of its strong silhouette, the chair adds structure to the room. I think it's important for guestrooms to be unisex, neither too masculine nor too feminine.

THOUGHTFUL GESTURES

Guestrooms shouldn't have family photographs in them or other items that are too personal. Your guests need to feel like the space is theirs. It's nice to provide a chair and ottoman with a reading lamp and current reading material, and it's also important to have bedside lamps. I like layering bamboo blinds with curtains so guests can have as much or as little light as they want. While the bedding should be inviting and luxurious, it should never be fussy. I spend the night in my guestrooms from time to time to make sure everything is functioning and comfortable.

When decorating a guestroom, keep an image of your favorite hotel room in the forefront of your mind

NEW YORK, NEW YORK
Rooms with a View

*W*hen Jim and I were asked by *House Beautiful* to design a show house in New York inspired by one of our favorite movies, we chose *Something's Got to Give*. Our goal was to create a sleek but inviting pied-à-terre that was a reflection of Jack Nicholson's clean, modern taste mixed with the softer style of Diane Keaton's Hamptons' beach house.

High up in a skyscraper, the apartment's staggering views had to be taken into account. There was just no way to compete with the sight of the Chrysler Building and the two rivers bordering Manhattan. So we brought in all the colors of the city—steel and concrete, the grays and creams of the old stone buildings, the blues of the rivers and sky—then softened and warmed them a bit. We took the city's energy and turned down the volume.

In the living room, a palette of ivory and sand, combined with blues and greens, creates a sophisticated look that is also serene. The soft, pale upholstery, silk curtains, and white cowhide rug layered on top of a wool carpet reflect the light with a soft sheen and absorb the sound. It is so quiet up there that you can hear a pin drop. You can see the city but not hear it. It is a true sanctuary.

A SHIMMERING SANCTUARY

I love to place glass and Lucite in front of windows because of the way they capture the light and sparkle. I especially love this pair of obelisks; the pagodas floating inside of them add an extra dimension. Simple, unified arrangements on tabletops keep things from looking cluttered.

A LIGHT-FILLED
CORNER

*The careful use of textiles
can create serene spaces. Curtains
are one of my favorite ways
to bring beauty and quiet into
a room. In the daytime, when
these curtains are open, natural
light flows in through floor-
to-ceiling windows, casting
an almost ethereal glow. The
pale colors of the upholstery
softly reflect it, while the
metallic table shimmers night
and day. I find that reflective
surfaces work well when combined
with a subtle color scheme.*

REPEAT A SHAPE
IN SUBTLE WAYS

*It's always challenging to design a
space that includes both a living
room and a dining room. They
have to relate to one another
while functioning as separate
areas. We chose upholstered chairs
in the dining area because we
thought they would unify it with
the living room. We also used
circular shapes—an oval pendant
light and table, round-backed
klismos chairs, and a curved
sofa—to create continuity. A
large, unpatterned rug connects
the spaces, and closely related
fabrics and colors complement
each other without competing.*

178

PLACING ART SUCCESSFULLY

LEFT: *In a small apartment, every piece of furniture has to have multiple functions. This mirrored console serves as a buffet for entertaining, and the nineteenth-century English benches tucked underneath can easily be moved to the living room or dining room for additional seating. An atmospheric painting by Shawn Dulaney hangs above the console.*

RIGHT: *The gridlike pattern in this painting by Doug Glovaski reminds me of windows on New York skyscrapers. The round forms of a mid-century Italian sculpture and mercury glass vase form a nice juxtaposition.*

The art we choose is a reflection of who we are—the more we look at it the more we discover about ourselves

UTILIZE EVERY SQUARE INCH OF SPACE

ABOVE: *This corner sofa softens the floor-to-ceiling windows and provides generous room for lounging in this small space. You can enjoy the views and a conversation at the same time.* RIGHT: *Jim designed this étagère to house the television inside a rosewood box. I like televisions to be out in the open, but I don't like seeing their sides or cords.*

THE DYNAMICS OF SYMMETRY

In this room, which doubles as an office and a bar, we hung black-and-white photographs of scenes from Paris and New York in an energetic symmetry. This distracts the eye from the low ceiling and makes the space instantly seem larger. I love tiny tables that hold just one drink exactly where you need it. I hate having to reach. Sit down, hold your drink out, and then place your table there. Be creative with coffee table choices—sometimes a small cube is all you need.

INVITE LIGHT IN

LEFT: *A round mirror finished in shades of silver and gold has a wonderful organic quality. It's almost a piece of sculpture.*
RIGHT: *The corner office has a stunning view of the Chrysler Building. The modern table-desk serves multiple purposes as a place to work, to read the newspaper in the morning, and to enjoy an intimate dinner for two at night. Generous wing chairs fill the space and give you plenty of room to sit back and cross your legs.*

Enjoying a magnificent view should not overshadow your everyday needs and wants

LAYER CURTAINS FOR DIFFERENT TIMES OF DAY AND NIGHT

This room was devoid of architectural features. To give it some visual interest, we used a subtly patterned wallpaper and wool carpet. Layers of wool curtains with sheers add texture as well as versatility for day- and nighttime living. In order to bring highlights into the room's monotone palette, we chose silver frames for the paintings and a silver-leaf border on the upholstered headboard. Although it was painted in the Hamptons by Cynthia Knott, the oil painting over the bed also captures the colors of dawn and dusk in Manhattan.

DAYBEDS OFFER GREAT VERSATILITY

ABOVE: *A double daybed allows this room to work both as a seating area and a spare bedroom. With ample cushions that can easily be stowed at night, it's perfect for lounging or sleeping. The Lucite coffee table floating in the middle of the small room keeps it from feeling crowded. Two upholstered chairs would have been too much for this room, so we combined an upholstered armchair with a painted wooden chair.* RIGHT: *Multiple textures of matelassé, painted cottons, and old-fashioned chenille all blend well together.*

Casual

he most common request I get from clients today is for a casual home. Carefree living in a house that's void of pretense—but not lacking in style—is everyone's dream. While nothing beats escaping to a beach or mountain house to decompress with friends and family, casual style need not be limited to weekends or summertime. After all, when we go home each day, wouldn't we all like to put on flip-flops and shorts and relax as if we're on a permanent vacation?

More than ever before, I find that clients want to live fully in each room of the house. They don't mind designated formal spaces, but there's a movement away from rooms that look assembled overnight to reflect a lifestyle and heritage that's not authentic. Let's face it: No one wants to live in a house that feels off limits, where the rooms might as well be roped off and guarded by docents.

Instead, people are looking for fresher, simpler style where the focus is on how to live, not just how to look pretty. Every room should be useable—and should be used without fear. Stripping away all that stuffiness and pretension opens the door to bolder decorating that creates a fun, laid-back

RELAX AND HAVE FUN

PREVIOUS PAGE: *Painted furniture is much more affordable than antiques or fine wood reproductions and creates a more relaxed environment. Because they are all painted white, the rounded forms of the mirror, brackets, and chairs in this dining room work together in a lively rhythm.*

Make your house an escape from

atmosphere. With a more free-spirited and open-minded approach to things like color and fabric, you can't help but feel more relaxed.

A hallmark of the casual house is kid- and dog-friendly furniture. But that no longer means style has to be sacrificed—I'm amazed at the quality of outdoor fabrics available today. Sturdy and stain-resistant, they are also surprisingly soft and stylish. They stand up well to wear-and-tear and are attractive enough for interior use. I like to use slipcovers in relaxed rooms because they have a looser look and can be taken off and washed. Painted wood coffee and end tables are also favorite choices because they can take it when people leave their drinks out—or even dance on them.

I like to bring outdoor elements inside casual houses. Anything made of natural fibers—wicker, rattan, raffia—brings everything down a notch. Whatever did we do without seagrass rugs? Casual, stylish, affordable (and therefore easily replaceable), they're appropriate in almost every setting, regardless of the room's style. For just a touch of something natural, arrangements of shells, wooden bowls, and glass pieces add organic notes without breaking the bank.

I know I've successfully created a casual environment when I see evidence that the house is lived in full tilt and to capacity. I love to see family rooms that look like twenty people were in there the night before watching movies. It's always great when clients ask for more barstools so people can cram around the kitchen island. To me, unfinished puzzles on game tables, stacks of magazines by chairs, and a fireplace with evidence of frequent use are not clutter, but signs that a house is well loved. Once I entered an old Shingle-style beach house I'd recently decorated for clients and found that tall stacks of paperbacks had replaced all the decorative objects I'd arranged on an old farm table. Right away, I knew it had been a great summer.

Decorating a casual home is all about embracing your lifestyle. Ask yourself how you really want to live, and then decorate in a way that reflects your answer. By expressing who you are instead of who you think you should be, you'll create an environment in which you and your guests can truly relax.

the harsh realities of everyday life

JOHN'S ISLAND
An Intracoastal Getaway

his house on the intracoastal waterway in Florida was designed as a second home for a family. Located right on the edge of the water, the house is filled with sparkle and light, which inspired the palette of clear, fresh colors primarily in hues of turquoise and green. In order to soften a wall of glass doors that overlooks the waterway, I designed aqua-colored curtains and a long valance with a scalloped edge that reminded me of waves. Because I knew there would be a lot of foot traffic from the pool just outside the doors, I used outdoor fabric with polyester trim that wouldn't be harmed by wet hands. It's also impervious to the fading and wrinkling that's inevitable with natural fabrics in the Florida climate.

The largest room in the house is a great room, that includes living and dining areas. My client is chic and stylish, but she didn't want anything too serious or stiff. She loves to entertain and wanted the room to be elegant enough for a cocktail party but relaxed enough for quiet family dinners. Painted wood and rattan furniture creates a crisp, clean look in the dining area, and in the living area, slipcovered sofas arranged around a coffee table large enough to rest your feet on invite relaxed gatherings.

USE REAL SHELLS

Raffia lampshades introduce natural texture and a warm tone into the great room, as do these flowers made from shells. In many Florida houses, people fall into the trap of using shell wallpaper, shell fabrics, shell everything. I steer clear of this, incorporating real shells instead. I was a shell collector as a child and have always been fascinated by them.

SATURATED COLORS BASK IN THE SUNSHINE

The impact of this wide valance sets the tone for a relaxed living room. The scalloped detailing at the bottom edge makes the room seem fun and inviting. Using bright colors in a limited palette and repeating colors in different patterns creates a cheerful and inviting atmosphere. Most people want to replace sliding glass doors with French doors, but in this case, the strong window treatment makes them disappear.

ELEMENTS OF NATURE

LEFT: *A pair of left and right chaises instantly puts you at ease when you enter this room. Relaxed and inviting, it's the perfect place to sit back and recap your day.*
RIGHT: *Assembling an assortment of natural objects is an easy way to accessorize on a budget. On this rattan étagère, baskets, coral, and shells mix with books, pottery, and glass to make an interesting statement.*

Casual decorating is driven by an attitude that is playful and carefree, never uptight or nervous

BANQUETTES ARE FUN

I always ask to be seated on a banquette in restaurants. It was my client's suggestion to arrange the dining room this way. We were both thrilled with the outcome. Pretty but practical, this seating area says, "We're going to have fun here." The sturdy teak table adds weight and volume, anchoring the room and playing off the whimsical elements of the decoration. Painting the rattan chairs put a new spin on an old Florida look.

TAKE TIME TO MAKE UP THE BED BEAUTIFULLY

ABOVE: *A painted chest and cloverleaf chair and a mother-of-pearl mirror combine to make a stylishly casual vignette.* RIGHT: *Shades of pale blue, light green, and ivory are repeated throughout the master bedroom in the furniture, fabrics, and framed botanicals. The upholstered headboard is elegant but relaxed, just like my clients. We chose sheets with a scalloped trim to add a feminine note. Good sheets are always worth the investment.*

TREASURED GETAWAYS
A Place to Relax and Unwind

An absence of technology, the presence of friends and family, and a connection to the world outside your windows are the mandates for a successful getaway. Getaways are places to unplug and turn off the world—and to eat, drink, laugh, and sleep, which are four of my favorite things to do. After you've spent a few days in a retreat that invites you to be carefree, unbuttoned, and unburdened by everyday restraints, then you're ready to face new challenges with a lighter heart and a clearer head.

One of the first getaways I can remember was to my paternal grandmother's house in Birmingham, Alabama. Every year, my four brothers and I would cram into the car for the long drive from Jacksonville. When we finally arrived, we'd race to the backyard where a bubbling mountain stream flowed through the property. We could not believe how cold the water was. I loved the feeling of the stones beneath my feet and would sometimes stand there until dark.

When a client in Birmingham asked me to design a pool house that would be used as a year-round retreat for family and friends, I tried to recapture that feeling by using slate and pebble stone floors. Combining stone with rough-hewn beams, bird prints, botanical motifs, and wicker, the interior reflects the beauty of the natural surroundings, creating a country escape in my client's own backyard.

LARGE SPACES CAN BE COZY

Simplifying your color palette makes it easier to combine patterns and textures. Within this slate gray and ivory palette, the humble materials of the driftwood lamps and wicker chair suddenly become stylish. White paint accentuates the exotic form of furnishings like these coffee and side tables.

PRACTICAL AND PRETTY

ABOVE: *Bird prints bring the outside in and a cabinet storing towels and boxes of sunscreen provides what you'll need when you head back outdoors to the pool.*
RIGHT: *This backyard retreat has all the elements you need for a getaway—lots of places to sit back and relax, plenty of side tables and reading lamps, and the right mix of style and comfort. All the seating is upholstered in outdoor fabrics that are attractive and practical. You can sit on any chair with a wet bathing suit on. Even the light-colored hemp rug can withstand the traffic of wet feet.*

ORDINARY INTO EXTRAORDINARY

LEFT: *In small spaces, imaginative choices have a lot of impact. A quirky antique washstand converted into a lavatory, lanterns used as sconces, and iron door hardware give this bathroom great style.*
RIGHT: *I chose pebble flooring in the kitchen because it reminded me of rocks in nearby streams, both in color and in its cool feeling underfoot.*

A small space is the perfect place for thoughtful, unexpected details

BALANCING CONTRAST

Show houses offer great opportunities to create fantasy rooms, like this sleeping porch I designed in Cashiers, North Carolina. Beginning with a very rustic space with natural stone, heavy timbers, and rough plank floors, I introduced a delicate iron bed, pressed white linens, a soft rug, and lots of fresh greenery. I wanted it to feel like a woodland retreat, but in a refined sort of way.

Don't be afraid to use
contrasting materials as long as
they balance one another

THE ESSENCE OF CASUAL LIVING
An Indoor-Outdoor Lifestyle

I was asked by *Coastal Living* magazine to decorate the ultimate beach house in a waterfront community called East Beach in Norfolk, Virginia. This beautifully planned neighborhood is a peaceful place where time seems to stand still and residents embrace an indoor-outdoor lifestyle. My goal was for the interior of the house to reflect this casual, relaxed way of life.

Every Wednesday afternoon, a sailing regatta passes in full view of the living room windows. Finding inspiration from the beauty of the sailboats, I chose items with nautical references. One of the first pieces was a wonderful round mirror with a frame made from boat paddles that forms a focal point in the adjacent dining room. Although the living room's blue, yellow, and white color scheme is bold and bright, pale blue walls and gauzy curtains of sheer, unlined linen capture the feeling of air and light on its perimeter.

Every part of the house, from the breakfast nook to the bedrooms, is designed to be carefree and approachable. This is a place to play cards, read books, and take a step back from hectic, overstimulated lives. Why watch television or play video games when you can walk to the beach, ride bikes, or watch the sailboats float by?

FRAME FUN OBJECTS

At an antiques show, I found thirty pairs of Bernardo flip-flops—all in size seven-and-a-half and all in perfect condition. I loved imagining their former owner—clearly a woman after my own heart when it comes to shoes! Restraining myself, I bought only four pairs that I later framed in Lucite boxes to hang in this seaside breakfast nook.

BE CREATIVE WITH DINING ROOM SEATING

PREVIOUS PAGE: *The bay window in the living room's corner overlooks amazing ocean views, so I designed an inviting window seat loaded with soft pillows to encourage lounging. Oversize armchairs and a sofa upholstered in crisp blue and white fabrics accented with pops of bright yellow make this space feel both tailored and fun.*
RIGHT: *I wanted the dining room table to seat up to ten people comfortably. To avoid using ten dining chairs, I arranged four slipcovered banquettes that each easily accommodate two people around the table. The bold color-block design of their slipcovers provides the visual punch the space needs. Using the same blue linen for the host chairs, I monogrammed the slipcovers with the letters eb for East Beach.*

LAYERS OF PATTERNS

LEFT: *A painting of bottle green waves by MaryBeth Thielhelm is the perfect addition to this seating area in the master bedroom. I had long admired it, so I was thrilled to place the painting here, where its graduating shades of green calm the pattern of the print.* RIGHT: *In the master bedroom, I hung an arrangement of kudu horns and ivory creamware plates above the bed. Three-dimensional arrangements of objects create visual interest and break up monotony. The curved silhouettes of the horns, valances, and headboard are in perfect visual harmony with one another.*

Using patterns in a big way doesn't have to make a room look busy

Comfortable

I'm a firm believer in three principles: beauty, practicality, and comfort. Without all three, any house falls flat. A practical house without beauty is completely lacking in interest. A beautiful house without comfort is a showplace, not a place for living. Comfort makes a house feel like home. But the question is, what makes a house comfortable? An enveloping reading chair or sofa that invites hours of lounging is part of it, but comfort is more than just furniture. When all the rooms in a house suit the needs of the people who live there, comfort naturally follows. And that means accommodating everyone—both homeowners and guests.

Every house needs at least one room, usually the family room or library, where people can sit anywhere and be at ease. There should be plenty of places to put your feet up, including the coffee table, and just as many places to put a drink down. Designing a comfortable family room is not all that difficult. The challenge is making it beautiful or handsome, as well. My male clients typically have one request: a big, comfortable chair. I say, give the man his chair! The two of you will spend

COMFORT NEVER SHOUTS—IT WHISPERS

PREVIOUS PAGE: *Placing a daybed instead of the usual console table in the foyer of this beach house instantly says, "Relax." For the upholstery, I mixed a variety of prints in closely related tones for an effect that's both lively and serene. Part of my first decorating project, this room landed on the cover of* House Beautiful.

The personality of the occupants needs to be expressed

more quality time together—and you can still have a say in what the chair looks like. If he wants leather, give him leather. If he asks for a recliner, try to talk him into a chair and ottoman.

In the living room, the challenge is reversed. It's expected to be a shimmering, elegant space—but no one wants to spend time in a room that feels too precious or delicate. Using furniture that brings a room down to human scale is one of the easiest ways to assemble a comfortable room. I prefer more chairs and fewer sofas because chairs are better suited for conversation. Slipper chairs are a great choice because they're easy to move around the room in different seating arrangements. You'd think that men would shy away from such small chairs, but they usually head straight for them. I've noticed that men love to sit on the edge of chairs and lean into conversations. The reality is that you don't have to use deep seating to make everyone feel at ease.

Textiles that engage the senses are another important aspect of comfortable rooms. My favorite upholstery fabrics are soft velvet, mohair, and chenille, because they invite touch and add an extra layer of softness. Subtle lighting is also essential. I like creating pools of light in rooms with plenty of table lamps. The effect is so much softer than overhead lighting.

Of course, whether or not guests feel completely at ease depends upon how welcoming your guest bedroom is. In addition to an inviting bed, a comfortable guestroom should have all the amenities of a hotel suite: luggage racks, a closet with empty hangers, a full-length mirror, a bedside carafe, and reading materials. Your guests should practically feel as though they could pick up the phone and order room service.

Throughout the house, comfort lies in the details. Every bedroom should have luxurious bedding to sleep on at night and a soft rug to step onto when you get out of bed in the morning. Bathrooms require fluffy towels and a tub you can sink into, and family rooms ought to have a sofa long enough to lie down on. When you enter your house, you should immediately feel at home. When you leave, you should feel rested. That is my goal.

in the decoration. It should look and live like they do

BLUE AND WHITE
Always Right

*F*lorida beach houses have to play hard. They need to be ready for wet bathing suits, damp dogs, and a large extended family of all ages spending time together. Everything in them needs to stand up to heavy wear-and-tear and at the same time be stylish, comfortable, and welcoming.

One of my favorite things about this house is the spool daybed in the entrance hall. My clients had a black Labrador retriever who liked to sit at the front door and greet people. I had the spool bed made with him in mind. It creates an unusual arrangement in the foyer that invites you to "Come on in and sit down."

A bright blue swordfish in the clients' collection inspired the house's color scheme. By mixing patterns with solids in similar shades of blue, I carried the bold colors of the swordfish throughout the house in its curtains, upholstery, and rugs. The choice of resilient, stain-resistant textiles suited the clients' lifestyle perfectly.

I decided to hang the swordfish in the dining room above a heavily carved and painted Italian console. A delicate Venetian chandelier in hues of blue hangs in the center of the room above a sturdy Irish drop-leaf table. This mix of whimsical and sophisticated elements, well-worn antiques, painted furniture, and sensible upholstery creates just the right balance of comfort and style through the house.

BOLD WALL COLOR CREATES A BACKDROP FOR ART

In this room, vibrant blue walls provide striking contrast with a white garden panel carved with a pattern of tropical foliage. Slipcovered upholstery, turned wood lamps, and painted rattan chairs make for a relaxed room. Wrapped in grass cloth, this coffee table is both stylish and indestructible.

IDENTIFY WHAT PLEASES YOU

RIGHT: *When I found this swordfish in my clients' other home, I said,*
"Come with me." Ranging from pale silvery blue to deep azure, the fish's
coloring provides the perfect palette for seaside living. A gossamer
Venetian-glass chandelier dresses up the dining room without weighing it
down. ABOVE: *In the family room, chairs upholstered in outdoor fabrics, a*
chevron-striped carpet, and Murano-glass lamps all pick up the tones.

TAKE A COLOR
AND RUN WITH IT

In the living room, a deep sofa and pair of swivel chairs are arranged for conversation. I use swivel chairs because their movement adds a level of comfort and versatility to a seating area. An oversize coffee table with a sturdy painted finish invites you to put your feet up and relax. Although the hues in the room are bright, the monochromatic palette creates a casual, breezy mood. Because the outdoor fabrics are easy to clean and the patterned carpet doesn't show dirt, everybody feels at home here, even the dogs.

ROOMS TO LIVE IN
Find Your Level of Comfort

*T*he number-one source of comfort in a room comes from the upholstery. Deep, plush, beautifully constructed upholstery that fits your body, your room, and your lifestyle is a necessity. The depth of the seat, pitch of the back, and arm height all have to be just right, which is why I always recommend sitting in a piece of furniture before you buy it.

In a comfortable house, everybody needs a place to sit and relax that suits him or her perfectly. It's important that there is plenty of room to circulate, a coffee table just the right distance from the sofa and chairs, adequate side tables and lamps, and upholstered pieces in varying styles and sizes. When there is a significant difference between the height of a husband and wife, I always choose seating with the taller person in mind. A tall person can never relax in a too-small chair.

I am convinced that curtains are perhaps the most essential ingredients for a comfortable room. They buffer noise, frame the windows, filter the light, and give a finished look. People sometimes complain that curtains are not a good investment because you can't move them from house to house, and that's true. But they also offer immense value. I would never live in a house without curtains.

UNITY OF COLOR INVITES COMFORT

RIGHT: *I love green in all of its variations. In this room, we combined wools, sheer stripes, cream cotton velvets, embroidery, cotton block prints, and silk fabrics, all in shades of green. Nothing matches exactly, but everything blends to create a comfortable, cozy room.* NEXT PAGES: *In a large room, I sometimes divide the space by placing sofas back to back. To create an environment that was both stylish and practical for a family with children, I covered the sofas in durable outdoor fabric.*

EMBRACE SYMMETRY

A generously proportioned sofa and plentiful pillows invite you to sit down and enjoy this space. Although this room is in one of our stores, it has the warmth of a welcoming home, with magazines to read, soft throws to wrap yourself up in, and flowers on the table. My customers always tell me how comfortable this room feels. We frequently find groups of shoppers sitting here, relaxing and visiting with each other.

ON A MOUNTAINTOP
A North Carolina Cottage

*M*y clients wanted to use this mountain cottage year-round, as a place to entertain friends in the warmer months and to enjoy quiet solitude in winter. It had to work equally well for relaxing dinner parties on the porch and cozy evenings by a roaring fire. Every space was going to be lived in and needed to feel comfortable and inviting.

Because this is a region that can be rainy and chilly, my clients requested a look that was lighter and brighter than typical mountain cabin interiors. While we agreed that the house needed to reflect its setting, we wanted to steer clear of buffalo plaids, antlers, twig furniture, or any other mountain clichés. I like to reference natural settings in more subtle, less specific ways. In this house, a palette of brown and green, faded floral linens, worn antiques, and hook rugs enhance the beautiful mountain views.

Light-colored walls of painted shiplap created a luminous quality that is equally inviting on cloudy and sunny days. The painted walls also provide the perfect backdrop for the clients' collections of glazed pottery, English transferware, and hunt engravings. It might seem backward to buy accessories before you build a house, but in this case, my clients' collections were so well selected that I could design around them. Finding a place for all their treasures made the clients feel instantly at home.

COLLECTED OVER TIME

Decorating with collections provides a sense of comfort by creating surroundings filled with familiar objects that reflect your taste. A set of English transferware established the palette for this sitting room, inspiring choices of upholstery in similar colors and patterns.

LOCAL MATERIALS SHINE

There is a spectacular mountain view outside these windows—the perfect counterpoint to this cozy, intimate room. Turned wood lamps and a rustic painted coffee table work together to give this living room a rich patina. Newly constructed houses can be made to feel as if they've been there for a very long time if you pay attention to the details. Elements in this cottage, including wormy chestnut mantels and distressed beams, reflect local building traditions and materials.

240

LET THE LIGHT IN

LEFT: *An English writing desk is put to work as a dressing table in this guestroom. Tucked into a dormer window, it's a nice place for guests to apply makeup or work on a laptop. I love the unusual shape of the vanity mirror.*
RIGHT: *The clients' collection of engraved hunt scenes were of special importance to them, so I hung them on the staircase walls where they are enjoyed on a daily basis. The asymmetrical composition of frames makes a powerful statement in the stair hall.*

Buying things we love is only the beginning
of the story—using them well completes it

TREAT THE OUTDOORS AS A ROOM

I like to decorate outdoor spaces as if they are rooms. Generally, I try to define areas for both sitting and dining. Careful measures should be taken to make sure the outdoor furniture is comfortable enough for long hours of sitting and visiting or unwinding over meals. Never use sets of outdoor furniture: I prefer to mix materials, combining painted wood, teak, wicker, and bamboo.

LEFT: *While I generally avoid using antlers in mountain houses, these made a graceful montage combined with the clients' collection of English transferware. Together, they create a pretty, three-dimensional arrangement on what otherwise would have been a big, blank wall.*
RIGHT: *In this guest bedroom, tones of green and white bring the beauty of the woodlands inside. The use of oversize checks enlivens the small space and seems to expand the room vertically and horizontally.*

Nothing says comfort more than an intimate, well-proportioned room

ART ON THE BEACH
Colorful Collectors

*T*his house in Atlantic Beach, Florida, belongs to a couple with whom we have been friends for twenty-five years. I'm always hesitant to work for friends, but this turned out to be one of the most satisfying jobs I've ever done. Both husband and wife have robust personalities that were reflected in the furniture and artwork they brought to the project. I knew that the decoration needed to be as stylish and dynamic as they are. Because this is an oceanfront house, the decoration also needed to be practical, so I used rugs and fabrics that were sturdy and could hold up well against sand and humidity.

My clients' collection of brightly colored contemporary art needed to be the center of attention, dictating the choice of white-painted wood walls. I love to decorate around art, rather than decorating a room then choosing the art last. In this case, I selected textiles with bold, fun colors and patterns that worked in energetic relationship with the surrounding artwork.

I am a neutrals person at heart, so I find it amusing that I have so many clients who love color. They have taught me to embrace it. I've learned to see color through their eyes and am amazed by how comfortable I am with it now.

MIXING MATERIALS

Hanging above an antique French buffet, this bold painting makes a strong statement. A mahogany table and iron chandelier anchor the bright dining room. Woven wood blinds soften the light and seagrass chairs with colorful outdoor fabric invite you to sit on them.

DON'T DESCRIBE YOURSELF, DEFINE YOURSELF

A painting by Yoon Jeong Lee led our choices for this room. We decided early on in the process that we were going to hang it here, and then chose fabrics, furniture, and rugs to complement it. The bold black-and-white striped rug, yellow club chairs, and green garden seats work well together with the energetic presence of the painting.

250

There is no stronger expression of joy in

LET COLOR LEAD

This room is very relaxed. All the chairs swivel, there is a big ottoman where you can rest your feet, and the upholstery is deep and plush. I chose a balance of soft and bright tones for the upholstery so the colors could stand up to the artwork without detracting from it. I had to insist that the clients paint the brick fireplace white. I love it when I'm right.

decorating than the uninhibited use of color

RESOURCES

ANTIQUES

Historical Americana
www.historicalamericana.com

A. Tyner Antiques
www.swedishantiques.biz

Robuck & Co.
www.robuckandcompany.com

Parc Monceau Antiques, Ltd.
www.Parcmonceau.com

Kenny Ball Antiques
www.kennyballantiques.com

Sentimento Antiques
www.sentimentoantiques.com

Lee Calicchio, Ltd
www.leecalicchioltd.com

John Rosselli Antiques
www.johnrosselliantiques.com

1st Dibs
www.1stdibs.com

Jonathan Burden
www.jonathanburden.com

Steven Postans Antiques
www.stevenpostansantiques.com

Bardith Ltd. Antiques
www.bardith.com

Newel, LLC
www.newel.com

George N Antiques
www.georgenantiques.com

Liz O'Brien
www.lizobrien.com

Howard Dawson Antiques
(607) 369-2027

GALLERIES

Sears-Peyton Gallery
www.searspeyton.com

Emily Amy Gallery
www.emilyamygallery.com

Sandler Hudson Gallery
www.sandlerhudson.com

Paul Kasmin Gallery
www.paulkasmingallery.com

Jackson Fine Art
www.jacksonfineart.com

J. Johnson Gallery
www.jjohnsongallery.com

Hagedorn Foundation Gallery
www.hfgallery.org

TEW Galleries
www.timothytew.com

DC Moore Gallery
www.dcmooregallery.com

Reynolds Gallery
www.reynoldsgallery.com

Wally Findlay Galleries
www.wallyfindlay.com

Wendt Gallery
www.wendtgallery.com

Spanierman Modern
www.spaniermanmodern.com

Stephen Haller Gallery
www.stephenhallergallery.com

RUGS

Stark Carpet
www.starkcarpet.com

Barrier Island Rugs
www.barrierislandrugs.com

The Rug Loft
www.rugloftdhurries.com

FABRIC

Ainsworth-Noah
www.ainsworth-noah.com

Ernest Gaspard & Associates
www.ernestgaspard.com

Grizzel & Mann
www.grizzelandmann.com

Jerry Pair
www.jerrypair.com

Travis & Company
www.travisandcompany.com

Lee Jofa
www.leejofa.com

Kravet
www.kravet.com

Rogers & Goffigon
(203) 532-8068

Pindler & Pindler
www.pindler.com

John Rosselli & Associates
www.johnrosselliassociates.com

FURNITURE

Hickory Chair
www.hickorychair.com

Baker
www.bakerfurniture.com

Century Furniture
www.centuryfurniture.com

Lee Industries
www.leeindustries.com

Mitchell Gold + Bob Williams
www.mgbwhome.com

Oly Studio
www.olystudio.com

Julian Chichester
www.julianchichester.com

Beeline Home
www.bunnywilliams.com/beeline

John Boone, Inc.
www.johnbooneinc.com

Dessin Fournir
www.dessinfournir.com

Dennis & Leen
www.dennisandleen.com

John Himmel Decorative Arts
www.johnhimmel.com

Nancy Corzine
www.nancycorzine.com/furniture.html

WORKROOMS

Highgrove Design
(704) 525-2130

Willard Pitt Curtain Makers
(404) 355-8232

J. Quintana Upholstery
(718) 361-0946

M. Southern Design Concepts
www.msoutherndesignconcepts.com

LIGHTING

Charles Edwards
www.charlesedwards.com

Vaughan
www.vaughandesigns.com

Visual Comfort
www.visualcomfort.com

Robert Abbey
www.robertabbey.com

TABLETOP

William Yeoward
www.williamyeowardcrystal.com

Simon Pearce
www.simonpearce.com

Mud Australia
www.mudaustralia.com

Dransfield & Ross
www.dransfieldandross.com

BEDDING

Matouk
www.matouk.com

Sferra
www.sferra.com

Pine Cone Hill
www.pineconehill.com

Peacock Alley
www.peacockalley.com

PHOTOGRAPHY CREDITS

Josh Gibson, Pages: Cover, 2, 5, 9, 12, 17, 18, 19, 20, 21, 22, 23, 25, 26, 27, 28–29, 30, 31, 32–33, 38, 39, 40–41, 44, 45, 50, 61, 62, 63, 64, 65, 66–67, 86, 91, 92–93, 94, 95, 96, 97, 98–99, 100, 101, 103, 104–105, 106, 107, 108–109, 110–111, 112–113, 114–115, 126–127, 128–129, 130–131, 133, 149, 151, 152, 157, 159, 160–161, 162, 163, 164–165, 166, 167, 168, 169, 170–171, 172, 173, 175, 176–177, 178–179, 180, 181, 182, 183, 184–185, 186, 187, 188–189, 190, 191, 212, 213, 222, 227, 228, 229, 230–231, 233, 236–237, 239, 240–241, 242, 243, 244–245, 246, 247, 249, 250–251, 252, 253

Erica Dines, Pages: 6, 68, 69, 116, 121, 122, 123

Mali Azima, Pages: 52, 56–57, 58, 59

Tria Giovan, Pages: 71, 72–73, 74, 75, 76–77, 78–79, 80, 81, 83, 84, 85, 215, 216–217, 218–219, 220, 221

Eric Piasecki, Pages: 135, 136–137, 138, 139, 140–141, 142, 143, 144, 145, 146, 147, 148, 150

Frances Spurling, Page: 82

Spencer Fisher, Pages: 192, 197, 198–199, 201, 202–203, 204, 205, 234–235

Howard Lee Puckett, Pages: 207, 208, 209, 210, 211

Roger Davies, Pages: 35, 36–37, 42–43, 46, 47, 48, 49, 51

Dominique Vermillon, Page: 200

Katharine Fuchs, Page: 125

Writing a book is quite a project, and there are a lot of people I would like to thank. First, I'd like to thank my publisher, Stewart, Tabori & Chang, for believing in me and my vision for this book. Thanks especially to my editor, Dervla Kelly, for her valuable input and insight.

I would like to say a heartfelt thanks to the people with whom I worked very closely on this project. Doug Turshen, my sexy book designer, has truly awed me with his style and talent. I've finally found a man I don't feel I need to micromanage. Thanks for everything Doug—and to your right-hand man Steve Turner, too. Thanks also to my coauthor, the talented Susan Sully, for taking my words and assembling them into something intelligible. I don't know how you do what you do—it makes my brain hurt!

I am hugely grateful to my wonderful staff. From the stores and warehouses to the office, we have a remarkable group of people working hard for us. Without them I would never be able to accomplish all that I do.

To the wonderful clients who have trusted me with their interiors, I offer a very special thank you. I'm so grateful for the opportunity to work with you, and for the friendships we have formed.

This book could not exist without the many talented photographers with whom I've worked over the years. Without your critical eyes and talent, these rooms would never have been captured in such a flattering light. I owe a special thanks to my good friend photographer Josh Gibson, with whom I've worked closely for many years.

I would like to thank my children Max, Ashley, Andrew, and Nellie Jane for growing up and moving out so I could finally make something of myself. Last, but most definitely not least, I'd like to thank my mother, Madeline. The confidence, independence, and work ethic she instilled in me have allowed me to grow and flourish. Fiercely intelligent and forward-thinking, she is both an inspiration and a blessing. Her unwavering support and encouragement mean the world to me.

Published in 2012 by Stewart, Tabori & Chang
An imprint of ABRAMS

Text Copyright © 2012 Phoebe Howard and Susan Sully

Library of Congress Cataloging-in-Publication Data:

Howard, Phoebe.
  The joy of decorating : southern style with Mrs. Howard / by Phoebe Howard.
    p. cm.
  ISBN 978-1-58479-961-0
1. Howard, Phoebe—Themes, motives. 2. Interior decoration--United States. I. Title. II. Title: Southern style with Mrs. Howard.
  NK2004.3.H69A4 2012
  747—dc23
        2011018747

Editor: Dervla Kelly
Designer: Doug Turshen with Steve Turner
Production Manager: Tina Cameron

The text of this book was composed in Requiem and Cochin.

Printed and bound in China
10 9 8 7 6 5 4 3 2

ABRAMS
THE ART OF BOOKS SINCE 1949

115 West 18th Street
New York, NY 10011
www.abramsbooks.com